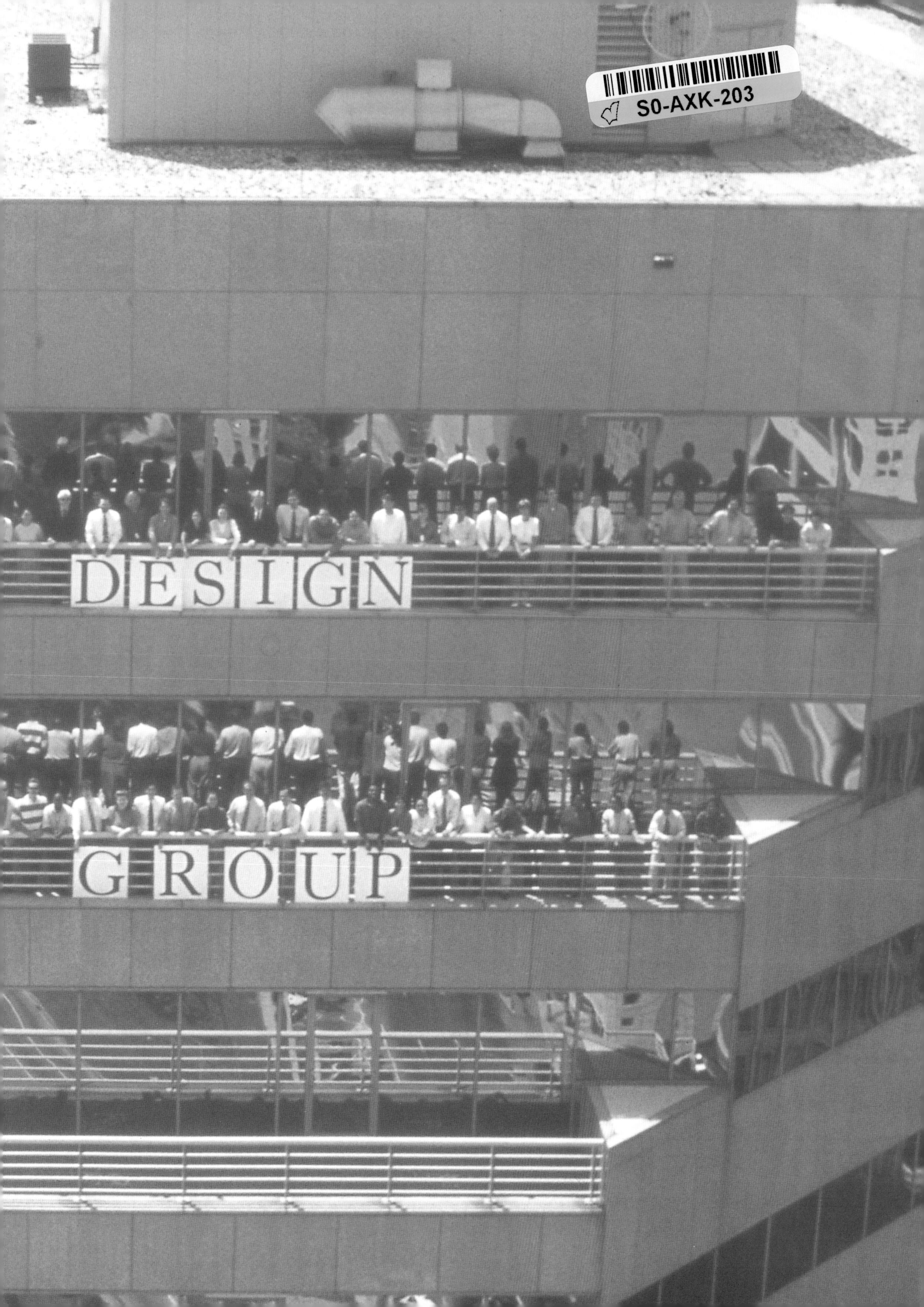
DESIGN
GROUP

THE MASTER ARCHITECT SERIES IV

Selected and Current Works

DEVELOPMENT
DESIGN
GROUP
INCORPORATED

First reprinted 2004
(The Images Publishing Group reference number: 582)

First published in Australia in 2001 by
The Images Publishing Group Pty Ltd
ABN 89 059 734 431
6 Bastow Place, Mulgrave, Victoria, 3170, Australia
Telephone: +61 3 9561 5544 Facsimile: +61 3 9561 4860
books@images.com.au
www.imagespublishinggroup.com

National Library of Australia
Cataloguing-in-Publication data

Selected and current works: Development Design Group Incorporated.

Bibliography
Includes Index
ISBN 1 86470 060 2

1. Architecture, Modern—20th century. (Series: The master architect series IV)
724.6

Designed by Valerie Knauff and Ahsin Rasheed
Coordination by Brian MJ Dame

Design production by The Graphic Image Studio Pty Ltd, Mulgrave, Australia
Website: www.tgis.com.au

Film by Ocean Graphics
Printed by Everbest Printing Co. Ltd. in Hong Kong/China

IMAGES has included on its website a page for special notices in relation to
this and its other publications. Please visit: www.imagespublishinggroup.com

Contents

Introduction

In 1987, a developer approached Roy Higgs and John Clark for help in creating a viable retail development in the Florida town of Coconut Grove, near Miami, USA. At the time, Coconut Grove was an eclectic art-and-poetry community whose bohemian nature added a considerable amount of local color, but it had never been able to sustain a sizable retail complex. In order to succeed, the new complex would have to be designed in ways that would attract people from nearby Miami, and that meant giving them something they could not get closer to home. "The challenge," says Higgs, CEO of Development Design Group, "was to take two acres of vacant land in an area where you couldn't attract retailers if you gave them the space, and show that with the right plan, the right merchandising dynamics, and the right urban design, it could work."

Higgs and Clark came up with an approach that challenged prevailing shopping-center conventions. In the late 1980s, a shopping center was generally one of two things: it was either a strip center with big-box anchor tenants, and smaller retail shops in a linear layout located next to a bleak expanse of asphalt parking lot, or it was a giant, enclosed mall, usually slick and contemporary, filled with small retailers, and anchored at the ends by large department stores.

The design for Coconut Grove would be neither. Drawing its inspiration from the villages of the Mediterranean, rather than prevailing, high-tech mall architecture, it called for a three-story, tile-roofed, U-shaped complex of boutiques, clubs, restaurants, and cafés surrounding an open-air, palm-tree-lined courtyard. "We intended," says Higgs, "to celebrate the climate of South Florida, not hide from it as was conventional wisdom." There would be no conventional anchor. Instead, a multi-screen cinema became the major drawcard, and circulation patterns were structured to take advantage of its atypical location on the top floor. When concerns grew about the viability of an approach that challenged so many conventions, Design Group took the bold and unusual step of forming its own leasing group to rent out the complex.

When it opened in 1990, Cocowalk, as the project was called, became an immediate success. In an industry that looked kindly on a sales average of $250 a square foot, Cocowalk's average soared to more than $800. It won a first-place award for innovative design from the International Conference for

Shopping Centers. It won an Award of Excellence from the Urban Land Institute. Most significantly, Cocowalk helped usher in the era of the urban entertainment center. "We made shopping an experience that deals with the senses," says Clark, Design Group's president. "People go there because it's an event."

History

Cocowalk helped firm up a growing reputation for the Baltimore, Maryland-based Development Design Group, which in 21 years has grown from two people and a secretary designing food courts for shopping malls into an international leader in planning, architecture, and design, with eighty-five employees at its home office in the United States and affiliate offices in Indonesia, Turkey, France, Mexico, and, most recently, South Africa. The company has succeeded not only because of its ability to design compelling environments, but also for its uncommon insight into the nature and future of commercial development.

Design Group traces its origins back to the American-based division of the Toronto firm Design International (DI). Higgs, a DI partner who had worked out of the firm's South Africa office, left South Africa in the late 1970s and opened the new American branch in Columbia, Maryland, near Baltimore. He and the handful of architects working with him got their first job—the renovation of a small delicatessen in Columbia Mall—in January 1979. Shortly afterward, Higgs hired Baltimore architect and former restaurateur John Clark to be his chief designer. After the departure of the others, the two were running the business on their own.

At Clark's urging the company relocated the office to Baltimore, a city undergoing an urban renaissance at the time. In the mid-1980s, with their business growing and design awards starting to come in, Higgs and Clark formed the quasi-independent DI Architecture. Their initial focus was on American projects, but when a late-decade recession slowed down development across the country, they expanded their range and began looking overseas for work. From their first international job—the planning and design of an arcade for downtown Amsterdam—this proved to be a highly profitable venture, and today more than 40 percent of Design Group's work, and a sizable percentage of its employees, come from outside the United States.

With business good and its reputation strong, Higgs and Clark saw the potential for growth. The company severed its connections with the parent firm, and in 1993 became Development Design Group, Inc.

Creative pragmatism

The label "architecture firm" is too limiting for Design Group. Their business is designing and creating places. And regardless of their professional credentials, the people who work there are designers, problem solvers who create engaging places that work for an exceptionally demanding clientele: results-oriented developers who require a project to succeed both aesthetically and commercially.

The scope of Design Group's work is broad, ranging from entertainment complexes, shopping centers, and hotels to resort communities, the creation of new towns, and regional master plans spanning thousands of acres/hectares that have the potential to revitalize national economies. The common thread in this work is commercial development, and Design Group's style is for big-picture development that combines far-ranging design expertise, a knack for innovation, and business and cultural understanding that anticipates the many ways in which a space will be used, and designs it accordingly.

Higgs and Clark set the ideological tone. Sit down with the two, and you quickly get a sense of their complementary skills and talents. One designs as he talks, sketching building façades, downtown streetscapes, and the layouts of new towns on the butcher paper covering the tabletop in Design Group's conference room. The other jots down bullet points as though he were preparing overheads for a business presentation. A wristwatch is set 15 minutes ahead, to help the firm get to the next big idea first. This mix of creativity and pragmatism defines Design Group, and is one of the chief reasons the firm has built a reputation both for its design expertise, and its business savvy.

Process

The commercial developers who come to Design Group have high, and sometimes conflicting, expectations. They want super-efficient places of commercial exchange built as cost effectively as possible, and then rented at top dollar. But they also they want places that will hold the consumer spellbound.

And the clients are not the only influence. A cartoon that is popular among Design Group employees illustrates the forces involved. It shows a shopping complex from the perspectives of a developer, a major tenant, environmentalists, customers, architects, and officials of the city in which the complex will be built. The developer sees a shopping center with a couple of large anchor stores at the nexus of exit ramps feeding in traffic from surrounding highways. The city officials see shops arrayed around a municipal plaza with a statue of city fathers at the center, and a public library and park nearby. The major tenant envisions a huge store—his store—surrounded by acres of parking. The customer sees slashed prices and a swimming pool, and the environmentalist envisions a greenspace with a river flowing between solar-heated stores.

The cartoon pokes fun at the conflicting demands of key stakeholders in a project, but not without revealing some very real underlying pressures. Ultimately, clients ask that a project be successful. But ensuring success means breaking through the myopia of any single perspective, and examining each project in the broadest possible context, considering the full range of forces that influence it—the business factors, political and economic realities, environmental concerns, the expectations of tenants who will rent the space.

Most important to Design Group is how the place will be used, for ultimately that is the key to commercial success. "I often like to ask architects what's most important about a building," says Higgs. "Some talk about its massing, or its fenestration, or its urban context, or the way it meets the ground. I tell them the most important part of a building is the door handle, because that's the first part you touch." Design Group looks closely at the people who will use the place they are designing, studying their culture and behavior, how they go about their lives, and how those patterns are likely to influence the building's use.

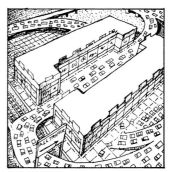
DEVELOPER

TENANT

ENVIRONMENTALIST

CUSTOMER

CITY OFFICIALS

An approach this thorough also means that Design Group takes an unusually active role in shaping the function of the places they design. Their planning phase considers not just the form of buildings and their relationships to one another, but also the merchandising mix, how different types of tenants can benefit from being near each other, how the appropriate blend of uses can help everyone involved. Complementary use is a consideration at every step, just as important when determining the height and scale of adjacent buildings as it is when asking whether a pet store really belongs next door to a restaurant. Finding the right mix of uses, in effect, becomes a key element of the design, and Design Group takes as much care in placing these fundamental building blocks as it does in the design of the structures and public spaces.

Theme

More often than not, design begins with a theme, an organizing principle that guides the project. Muvico Theaters asked Design Group to create a cinema complex in Davie, Florida, a community less than 20 miles from Miami and Fort Lauderdale, but in a setting that makes it feel distant and remote. Designers sought inspiration from remote places: wilderness, oceans—finally settling on the desert. After melding the desert concept with the grandeur associated with great theater, they arrived at an Egyptian theme and a design evoking a pharaoh's temple.

The theme gave an organizing logic that filtered down through every design layer, informing creative and analytical decisions. The design was bold, bordering on outlandish, but like good cinema, carried out with an attention to quality and detail that causes moviegoers to suspend disbelief and enjoy the fantasy world they have entered. Within weeks of its opening in the spring of 1999, Muvico Paradise 24 became one of the top ten highest-grossing theaters in the United States, and it has remained there ever since. "It had to be done well enough that it didn't come off as a farce," says Clark. "The quality had to be there."

Uncommon diversity

At a time when the work of many firms tends to carry the imprint of one or two signature architects, Design Group, as its name would suggest, finds its strength in the group. There is no one design director, no one master architect, no one signature style. The firm is not Higgs & Clark, but 85 creative individuals from more than 20 countries and speaking over 25 languages who are part of a team that brings a diversity of perspective, professional training, and life experience that few other firms can match. From this diversity comes creative tension—a tendency to question and a tendency to consider new possibilities—that improves a design.

Its extraordinary diversity also means that Design Group can bring more than the usual amount of insight to design challenges anywhere around the globe, and can apply ideas learned from one cultural milieu to another. Designers who grew up in Turkey, or Indonesia, or the Middle East, bring special awareness of such things as the orientation of buildings with respect to religious symbols, the significance of traditional tile patterns, or new ways to use indigenous materials. One influence the firm has imported from another culture—Feng Shui, the ancient Chinese art of creating and arranging environments—is as applicable to the firm's numerous projects throughout Asia as it is for work in other parts of the world. The firm's success in places as different as Europe, Asia, Africa, South America, and the United States results in large part from the understanding of those regions its employees can bring to the table.

Work

This diversity makes it hard to pinpoint any signature style in Design Group's work. Easton Town Center, in Columbus, Ohio (USA), creates the feel of small-town middle-America through vernacular building designs, careful attention to scale and mass, and adherence to a rigid, European-style street grid. In contrast, designs for Toronto's Cornell Town Centre or South Africa's Zonk'izizwe Master Plan depart from the grid with a curvilinear layout that reflects influences from Africa and the Middle East. Colonial Plaza, a mixed-use complex in Caracas, has the warmth and ambiance of a 17th-century Spanish Colonial hill town, while Johannesburg's The Zone@Rosebank, with its supercharged streetscape of billboards, ad panels, and graffiti, is loud, high-tech—an ultra-contemporary, urban entertainment center.

This range of design solutions makes the firm attractive to developers looking to breathe new life into commercial structures that are showing signs of age. By carving the middle out of Cape Town's Cavendish Square shopping center, and giving it a dramatic exterior facelift, the firm transformed a hulking city box into a thriving urban retail complex. Burlington Mall, in Massachusetts (USA), was 22 years old when Design Group undertook an interior and exterior overhaul, and added a new second level with 12,000 square meters (127,000 square feet) of additional retail space. In Pretoria, South Africa's capital city, one of Design Group's most ambitious renovation projects involves doubling the size of the Menlyn Park retail and entertainment center by adding additional retail floors. The redesign adds such features as a sports-and-entertainment arena, and a drive-in movie theater atop a parking garage, while covering a three-level court carved from the complex's center with a tensile roof.

Sometimes it is an entire region that is in need of new energy. The firm has developed revitalization plans for cities as different as Washington, DC, and Johannesburg, South Africa, and has designed new cities and communities with the potential to invigorate national economies.

Along the way, Design Group has changed some conventional thinking about commercial design. Industry wisdom held that a shopping center needed a department store anchor, until Cocowalk succeeded with a cinema complex as its main attraction. The firm adds interest and variety by mixing in street merchants and farmers' markets with designer boutiques in upscale shopping centers. Open-air retail-and-entertainment centers offer relief from enclosed box malls. Graphics and other elements sometimes play as important a role as architecture in defining an environment. And though you would be hard-pressed today to find a mall without a food court, that wasn't the case when the firm started designing them.

If there is a common signature in Design Group's work, it is a signature of approach to design more than design itself. Its consistent attention to tenant goals, merchandising strategies, and the desires of the people who use the places being designed. And its understanding that a built environment can be more than a place to shop, or work, or eat, or sleep. "It's about the experience of being in a place," says Clark. "It's life as theater."

Recognition

By just about every standard, Design Group's story is a success story. The Group has designed projects for virtually every corner of the globe, and its work consistently performs at levels well above accepted measures of commercial success. An unusually high proportion of the projects it designs are built. The Group's clients are satisfied, as their high number of repeat clients bears out. The firm has won more than 60 international design and planning awards in the past 10 years alone, from FIABCI, the International Council of Shopping Centers, the Pacific Coast Builders Conference, and the Urban Land Institute, among others.

If there is any frustration in all this, it comes from what the firm sees as the tendency of mainstream architecture critics to pass over commercial development in favor of higher-visibility, urban landmark structures such as office towers and museums, many of which fail to live up to expectations. "When you look at the architectural monuments that are regarded as classics," says Higgs, "you find many that are held up as great pieces of architectural splendor, but that fall short in how they're used by real people in the real world. If a place doesn't work for those who'll use it, what's the point of having it?"

Part of the problem may come from the fact that many critics look at so-called themed architecture, which makes up a sizable portion of the Design Group portfolio, as artificial, as something less than real architecture. But themed architecture, Higgs notes, goes way back, back as far as the Grand Bazaar of Istanbul, the world's first shopping center.

And like the Grand Bazaar, the places Design Group designs make their loudest statement by what goes on in them, by how they are used. Like all good architecture, the Group's work is sensitive to proportion, scale, mass, texture. But it is also animated, filled with color and light, designed to generate excitement, enjoyment, fun. "We don't design monuments," Higgs says. "We don't build monuments. What we build has to work in the real world."

Vision

Being successful means staying on top of forces shaping that real world. We live in an era when our lives have become more complex, and time itself has become a precious commodity. New technologies and the Internet bring rapid access to information, communication, goods, and services at our fingertips, causing some futurists to predict the end of commercial exchange as we know it. The pace of life has grown more frenetic.

Design Group succeeds because it is able to anticipate the next cultural wave as it is building out at sea, well before it crests, breaks, and rolls up on the beachhead of contemporary society. If time is a commodity, riding that wave means recognizing that the most sought-after places will be those that allow people to make the greatest use of limited time. If we can buy a product with the click of a mouse, riding that wave means knowing that places designed for the exchange of goods and services must offer something more if they are to coax us away from our computer screens. As the pace of life grows faster and we feel out of control, it means seeing that we long for a simpler past.

The firm understands that we are moving into a time when architects as we know them may cease to exist, with places designed and created by many people and influences. Trained architects are still one of those influences, but so are engineers, town planners, lighting designers, entertainers, the media, graphic artists, lifestyle consultants, and the tenants who will use the places. "In a dramatic way," says Higgs, "it will not be the producer but the process of commerce itself that will craft the environment in which it thrives."

Portfolio

The 76 projects profiled here span 21 years and six continents. They range in size from the graphic elements and décor of a trade-conference booth for the New York-based International Council of Shopping Centers, to the 10,000-hectare (25,000-acre) Pantai Kapuknaga urban Master Plan in West Java, Indonesia. They reflect Design Group's range of expertise in design, architecture, planning, urban design, and graphic arts.

Most of all, what this diverse range of work shows is how Development Design Group has used design to attract, stimulate, entertain, persuade, satisfy, and engage people in the rich and multifaceted experience of being in a special place.

Richard Bader writes about art, education and design from his home in Baltimore, Maryland, USA.

CAVENDISH SQUARE

AKMERKEZ ETILER

BUR JUMAN CENTRE

COCOWALK

EASTGATE

MONTROSE CROSSING

WESTGATE

OLD ORCHARD

PARADISE RETAIL

ALDHIYAFA

WAREHOUSE ROW

FESTIVAL PARK

RETAIL

Cavendish Square

Design/Completion: 1996/1999
Cape Town, South Africa
Old Mutual Properties
Local Architects: Stauch, Vorster
Architecture, Inc.
878,365 square feet/81,600 square meters
Reinforced concrete base, steel parking
deck
Masonry with stucco

The renovation of Cavendish Square, a three-level shopping complex set against the dramatic natural backdrop of Cape Town, reinvigorated a shopping center that was in danger of failing. Prior to the renovation, what existed was a stark, imposing, inward-focused, two-level center that was desperately in need of new life. The redesign opened up the building, turning it inside out and integrating it with the surrounding street. An exterior facelift rounded severely angled insets and added display windows, distinctive torch-shaped street lighting, and bright banner graphics in gold, turquoise, and violet. Three-dimensional advertising panels also helped energize the streetscape. A striking skylight entrance and new canopies mark entry demarcations, bringing visitors and light into a central court.

Inside, the dominant feature is a new atrium, carved out of the middle of the building, that rises through the shopping levels and through three levels of parking to a rooftop skylight. The atrium and skylight bring daylight inside and tie together a complex that includes a department store, retail stores, a food court, and a 16-screen cinema complex. A garden surrounds the atrium cylinder on the lowest parking level. Natural wood, indigenous plants, African colors and patterns on floors and walls, and warm tones throughout reflect the character of the surrounding area. The regional influence even carries down to details like the brass elephant-head supports for glazed balustrade railings.

ICSC Design Award – Renovation or expansion of an existing project, 1999
DuPont Benedictus Certificate of Recognition – Innovation in Architectural Laminated Glass, 1998

1

2

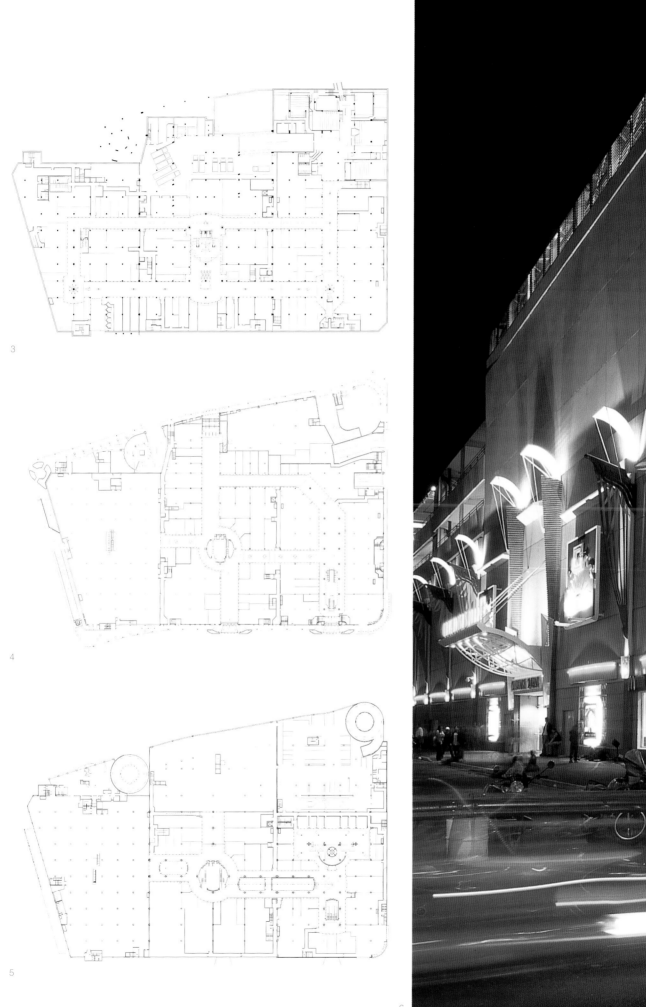

3

4

5

6

7

8

9

Imagery:	1	Dreyer Street entry
	2	Feature canopy entrance
	3	Lower level plan
	4	Street level plan
	5	Upper level plan
	6	Dreyer Street façade
	7	Cavendish Court
	8	Details at Cavendish Court
	9	Typical lower level mall
	10	Restaurant court ceiling
	11	Cavendish Court atrium section
	12	Cavendish Court from above
	13	Feature elevators at Cavendish Court

10

12

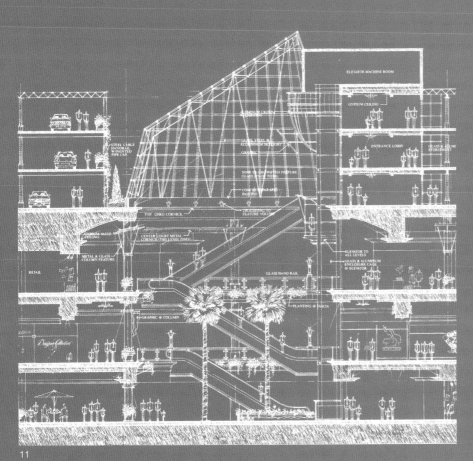

11

13

Akmerkez Etiler

Design/Completion: 1991/1994
Istanbul, Turkey
Partnership of Akkok Group, Tekfen and
Dogu-Bati
440,000 square feet/40,900 square meters
Reinforced concrete superstructure
Masonry with stucco and stone veneer,
glass curtain wall system

Imagery: 1   Exterior façade
              2   Typical plan
              3   Food court
     Opposite   Entrance from street

The metal and granite façade of Akmerkez's shopping-center base and the blue-glass exteriors of its towers create a distinctive urban landmark in the Etiler area of Istanbul, while having the practical advantage of being able to withstand the city's harsh environment and pollution. Akmerkez integrates a four-story retail, dining, and entertainment center with three office/residential towers in a contemporary architectural style. A wide ground-level sidewalk promenade, a sculptural overhanging canopy, and a three-meter setback at the terrace level have all been designed to minimize the visual impact of the building's height.

Inside, Akmerkez contains department stores, smaller retail establishments, restaurants, a 1,000-seat food court, and a multiplex cinema. The dominant features are three distinct interior courtyards – one beneath each of the towers – that take advantage of the site's unusual triangular shape and help both orient visitors and influence their movement through the complex. An asymmetrical skylight, dramatic lighting, prominent columns clad in polished stainless steel, and other design features draw visitors' attention upward to a roof garden and promote movement among levels.

ICSC Design and Development Award – Innovative design of a new project, 1996 *ICSC First Place Design Award* – Best new shopping center in Europe, 1995 *FIABCI Prix d'Excellence finalist* – Retail properties, 1997 *DuPont Benedictus Certificate of Recognition* – Innovation in Architectural Laminated Glass, 1998

1

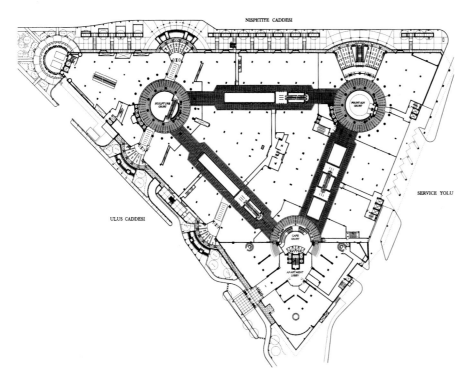

2

3

Bur Juman Centre

Design/Completion: 1991/1992
Dubai, United Arab Emirates
Al Ghurair Group
Local architect: Schuster, Pechtold &
Partners, UAE
811,026 square feet/75,374 square meters
Reinforced concrete, pre-cast façade,
structural steel roof terraces
Marble flooring, glass skylights

Site constraints posed a major challenge in designing Bur Juman, a premier multi-level shopping complex on the outskirts of Dubai. The solution was to create a three-level center that adopted an unusual double-mall scheme, with two parallel malls linked by a center court and two end courts. A second challenge came from the client's desire for natural light in a scorching desert climate. The design introduces to the region the first uninterrupted, tinted, double-glazed skylights, whose energy efficiency significantly reduces heat transfer. In order to create large, open areas and to take advantage of natural light, the designers used steel truss construction, another new concept in a country where poured concrete is the norm. A roof air-conditioning system transmits cooled air across the skylight to cool the entire mall. To compensate for the expense of the glass for the skylights, builders took such resourceful steps as using sand excavated in laying the foundations in creating the aggregate for the pre-cast concrete façade.

The main shopping area houses large anchor stores, a supermarket, a food court, and numerous small shops and boutiques. All tenants open onto either a court area or a mall – a new concept in a country used to back-corridor store locations. The marble floor and exterior façade use designs that are contemporary variations of traditional Islamic motifs. Plans are underway to expand the center.

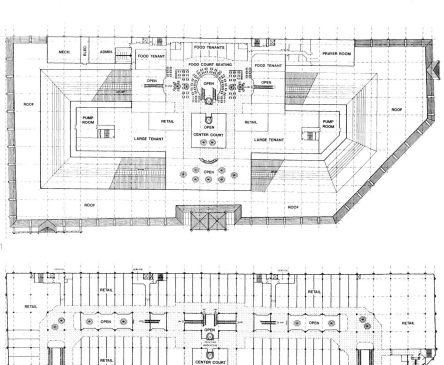

1

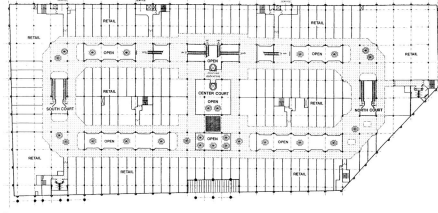

2

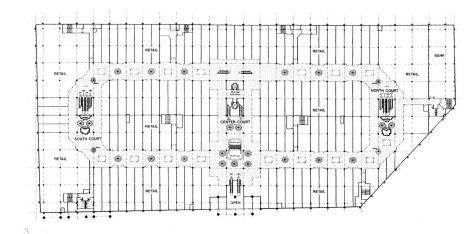

3

4

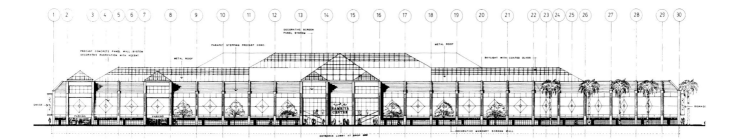

5

Imagery:
1 Second floor
2 First floor
3 Ground floor
4 Upper mall view
5 East elevation
6 Food court
7 View from mezzanine level
8 View from Trade Center Road

6

7

8

Cocowalk

Design/Completion: 1987/1990
Miami, Florida, USA
Constructa Properties & Grand Oak
Partnership
200,000 square feet/18,590 square meters
Post-tensioned concrete
Masonry with stucco finish, natural stone
and pre-cast concrete accents

As the first themed, urban retail-and-entertainment center in the USA, Cocowalk, in Miami, Florida, has played a key role in defining the genre. Its three U-shaped levels contain more than 40 shops, restaurants, nightclubs, and cafés, and a 16-screen multiplex cinema. Parking under and behind the center enters directly into shopping levels.

One innovation was making the cinema the project's anchor; another was locating it on third floor, with walkways structured to draw moviegoers past other merchants. Still another innovation is Cocowalk's reduced scale, with floor-to-floor heights at about 4 meters (12 feet), roughly two-thirds of the norm in the United States. The smaller scale increases intimacy and interaction within and between levels.

Cocowalk's centerpiece is a palm-tree-lined, open-air courtyard that doubles as a food court and entertainment venue. Boutique-lined verandas on all levels surround the courtyard, which opens directly to a perimeter sidewalk, so visitors can enter the complex without committing to parking lots, vestibules, or even stores. Red roof tiles and stucco siding give Cocowalk the look and texture of a Mediterranean village, and are in keeping with its South Florida environment. Details such as the selection of 15 different kinds of floor tile, and a variety of building elevation designs create the impression that the complex has evolved naturally over time.

FIABCI Prix d'Excellence – retail properties, finalist, 1997

ICSC Design and Development Award – Innovative Design of a New Project, winner, 1992

Urban Land Institute Award of Excellence – small-scale commercial/retail development, 1992

National Mall Monitor Centers of Excellence, honorable mention, 1991

City of Miami, Beautification and Environment Award, 1991

Imagery:
	1	Overall model
	Opposite	From above Grand Avenue
	3	Virginia Street banners
	4	Street-level plan
	5	Second-level plan
	6	Third-level plan
	7	Cinema-level plan
	8	Terrace detail
	9	Virginia Street façade
	10	Entry fountain

1

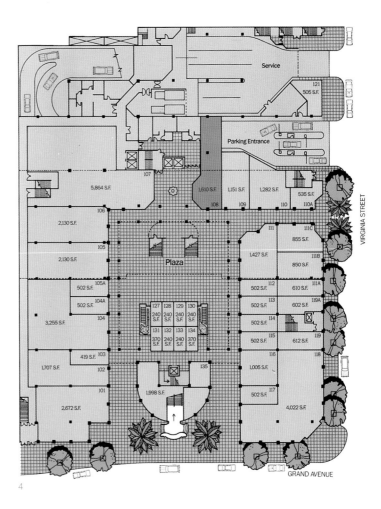

4

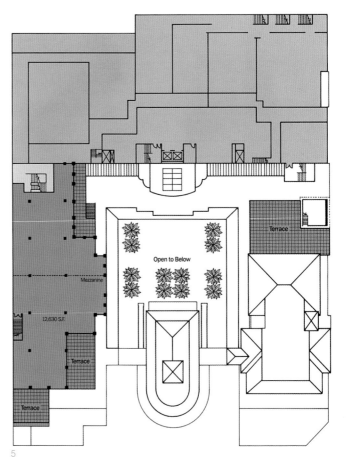

5

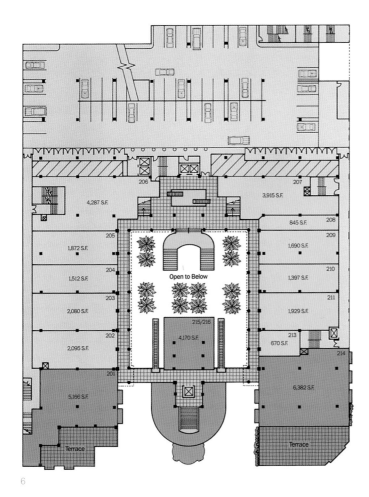

6

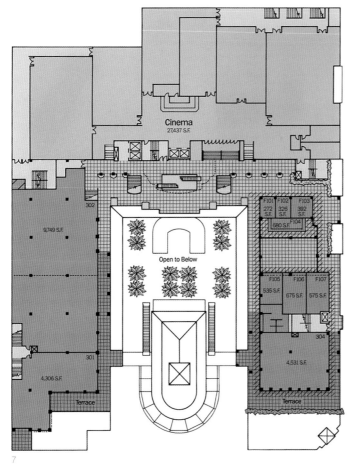

7

8

9

10

11

12

13

14

Imagery:

	11	View from Grand Avenue
	12	Dining in courtyard
	13	Central Plaza
	14	View from across Grand Avenue
	15	Tower entry from Virginia Street
	16	View toward north plaza façade
	17	Cinema plaza steps
	18	Courtyard façade

15

16

17

18

Eastgate

Design/Completion: 1992/1996
Harare, Zimbabwe
Old Mutual Properties
Local architect: Pearce Architectural
Partnership
55,359 square feet/5,145 square meters
Reinforced concrete, hollow plank concrete
with integral air plenum
Masonry exposed brick with pre-cast
accents, glass and steel roof with steel
bridge structure

FIABCI Prix d'Excellence – retail properties, category winner, 1998

DuPont Benedictus Certificate of Recognition – Innovation in architectural laminated glass, 1998

ICSC (International Council of Shopping Centers) Certificate of Merit – innovative design, 1997

Steel Award South African Institute of Steel Construction – excellence in the use of structural steel, 1997

Fulton Award, The Concrete Society of Southern Africa – excellence in the use of concrete, 1997

Surrounded by the at-times intimidating traffic of downtown Harare, Zimbabwe's capital, the Eastgate retail and office complex captures the urban street energy within the comfort and security of a contemporary public plaza. The complex is the shopping base for a two-building, nine-story, environmentally responsive commercial center designed by Harare's Pearce Partnership. Design Group was responsible for the shopping and public spaces.

The design removed a city street that bisected the block and created a two-story shopping mall two blocks in length along a 145-meter (160-yard) atrium between the office buildings. The shopping area is covered and open-air. The 50 shops are mostly small and locally owned (there is no traditional retail anchor), and are designed in an interesting pop-out storefront manner. Open to downtown streets at both ends, the mall has theater stages, fountains, and other features near each end to attract visitors. A food court, the first in Zimbabwe, draws visitors to the upper shopping level.

A dominant feature is a glass-block pedestrian bridge running the length of the atrium. Its latticed beams use technology found on the Zambezi River's historic Victoria Falls Bridge. Special bridge lighting and the glass-block floor create a stunning effect, especially at night. Indigenous foliage planted on ledges and overhangs is taking root, softening elevations and copying the forest canopies and rock overhangs common throughout the region.

Eastgate has become a model of urban commercial viability, serving both as a popular shopping center and as a community destination for the citizens of Harare.

1

JASON MOYO AVENUE

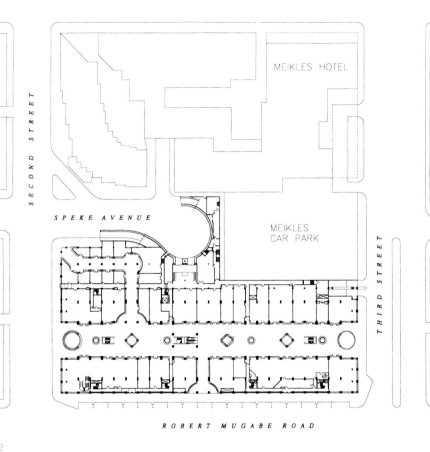

MEIKLES HOTEL

SECOND STREET

SPEKE AVENUE

MEIKLES
CAR PARK

THIRD STREET

ROBERT MUGABE ROAD

2

3

4

Imagery: 1   Central atrium
           2   Site plan
           3   Shopping level
           4   Building model
           5   Store fronts

5

Montrose Crossing

Design/Completion: 1994/1998
Rockville, Maryland, USA
GFS Realty
115,000 new square feet/10,688 square meters
Steel frame
Brick and pre-cast concrete block, split-face concrete block, exterior insulation systems

1

Montrose Crossing transforms a conventional, nondescript strip mall in this growing community near Washington, DC, into a contemporary retail and entertainment "neighborhood" laid out on an urban grid. One key to the project's success was improving access. The design extended Chapman Avenue, a busy thoroughfare near even busier Rockville Pike, so it would run through the middle of the site. In order for Montrose Crossing to remain competitive, the former one-level center grew to two levels in most places, and four levels in some locations. On-street parking and a new

parking garage eliminate the acres-of-blacktop approach common to many conventional shopping centers.

A redesigned footprint creates a town-center shopping complex, with big-box merchants, department stores, and smaller retail and dining establishments arrayed on a grid of pedestrian-friendly streets. Outdoor furnishings, colorful awnings, banners, new lighting and landscaping, and other additions, such as mosaic tile paving and a commissioned public artwork, invigorate the streetscape. Illuminated rooftop domes are among the more prominent changes to the

buildings. Another significant change was to design buildings with a 360-degree exposure, eliminating unattractive "back side" views.

The transformation of Montrose Crossing is part of an evolving community master plan, which aims to relieve traffic congestion and create a greater sense of identity for the region. The next phase involves additional retail.

ICSC Design and Development Award – Certificate of Merit, Renovation/expansion of an existing project, 2000

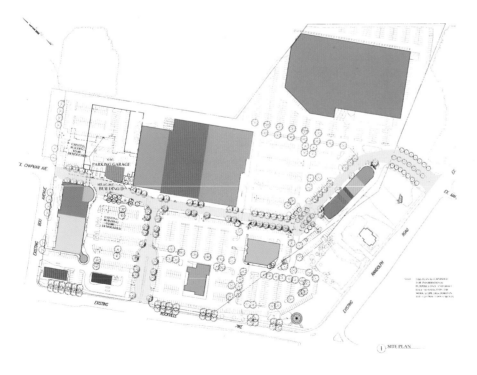

2

Imagery:
1 New retail building
2 Site plan
3 Entry drive
4 New two-level retail

3

Westgate

Design/Completion: 1990/1997
Harare, Zimbabwe
Old Mutual Properties
Local architect: Clinton & Evans Associates,
Harare
448,541 square feet/41,686 square meters
Reinforced concrete with steel roof
Masonry back-up finish and pre-cast,
handpainted glazed-tile accents

Westgate creates a new retail and entertainment community center in the rapidly expanding suburb of Bluff Hill, outside of Harare. It introduces Zimbabwe to a town-center concept that has grown popular worldwide. Located on regional bus transport routes, Westgate is part of an overall master plan that also calls for residences, schools, and office space.

Westgate is designed as a series of linear pedestrian shopping streets connecting landscaped plazas and courtyards. The open-air streetscape takes advantage of the region's ever-present sunlight and temperate climate. The tenant mix accommodates everything from large national retailers to the informal merchants and street traders common to the region. It includes more than 100 boutiques, a supermarket, a fresh food hall, and a multiplex cinema, combining shopping and entertainment opportunities to attract a multicultural cross-section of visitors from across income levels.

Westgate's centerpiece is a two-story, five-sided retail complex. An outdoor plaza and fountain mark the entrance, and the interior courtyard is a garden and tea pavilion.

Careful attention to landscaping links the center to its natural surroundings, as do prominent sun, moon, wind, and cloud graphic design elements, which have the additional advantage of helping to orient visitors.

Westgate was designed and built during an economic recession. Thanks to careful attention to concept, design development, and the merchandising mix, it has proven to be not only a commercial success – with a long waiting list of prospective tenants – but an important community anchor.

ICSC Design and Development Award – Innovative design of a new project, 1998

Imagery:	1	Expansion plan
	2	East mall
	3	Elephant court
	4	Parking entrance
	5	Overall perspective
	6	Cinema court
	7	West mall
	8	View from parking

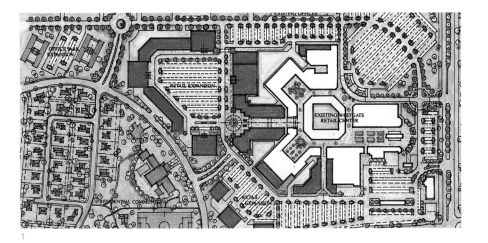

1

2

3

4

6

7

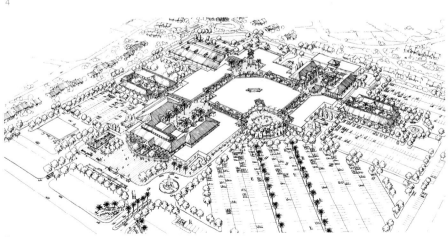

5

8

Old Orchard

Design/Completion: 1992/1995
Skokie, Illinois, USA
JMB Urban Development & Equity
Properties
Total: 1,800,000 square feet/167,286 square
meters
Expansion: 500,000 total square feet/46,468
square meters
Steel frame
Brick, stucco, metal roof, custom ironwork
and pre-cast stonework

Old Orchard involved the renovation and expansion of a formerly successful north-Chicago shopping center in ways that created an atmosphere of adventure and play while restoring the center's popularity. The former center, a disconnected assemblage of fading stores, was unable to compete with more contemporary, multi-use malls and shopping complexes in the area.

The chief design challenge was to give interest and variety to a long, linear, open-air site. With the new design, a promenade links a series of gardens, plazas, and courtyards, each with its own theme. One garden has stone animals and fantasy creatures, some draped with foliage "blankets" where children climb and play. Fountains and water dominate another area, a quiet pond another, and a rose garden still another. The use of texture, form, scale, and color makes the gardens attractive four seasons a year, even in the occasionally harsh Illinois winter climate. The different themes add a sense of discovery, make traveling the length of the complex fun, and help to orient shoppers as they move among the retail stores surrounding the interior. Before the renovation visitors had to go through other stores or into a parking lot to move from one end of the mall to the other; now each establishment has a storefront that opens on an interior plaza or courtyard. Two new premier department stores anchor the complex at either end. Cinemas and food courts add variety to the shopping experience.

ICSC Design and Development Award – Renovation/expansion of an existing project, 1997

FIABCI Prix d'Excellence – retail properties, finalist, 1997

Imagery:
1 Massing model
2 Pear Avenue Mall
3 Entry from parking
4 Formal garden
5 Informal garden
6 New Bloomingdale's court

1

2

3

4

5

6

7

8

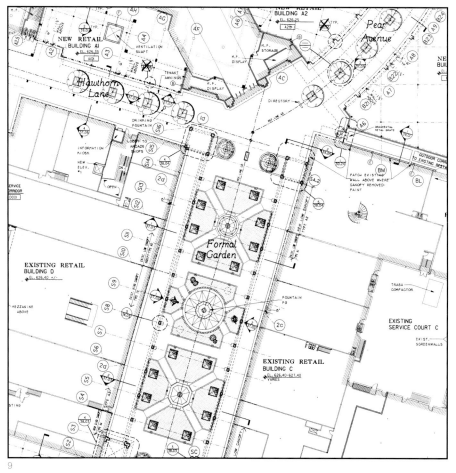

9

10

13

11

14

Imagery:

7   The Nordstrom garden
8   Pear Avenue Mall
9   Formal garden site plan
10 Professional building fountain court
11 Fountain court towards south
12 Site plan
13 Vineyard entry court from parking
14 Renovated arcade

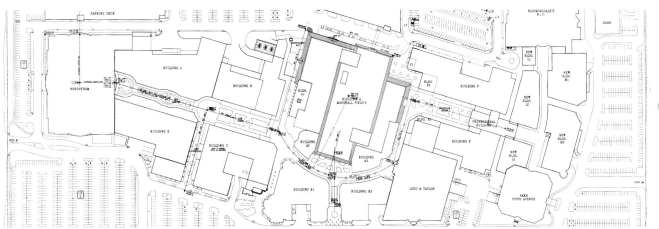

12

Design/Completion: 2000/on-going
Davie, Florida, USA
Muvico Theaters
100,000 square feet/9,294 square meters
Masonry bearing walls/steel frame
Exterior finish insulation and GFRG (Glass
Fiber Reinforced Gypsum)

Paradise Park is designed to become the retail complement to Muvico Theaters' highly successful, Egyptian-themed Paradise 24 cinema complex in Davie, Florida. Together the two would form a major retail and entertainment center for the area, with the movie complex and retail center facing each other along an interior roadway that accommodates cars and pedestrians.

Where the Paradise 24 cinema recreates an Egyptian temple, Paradise Park captures the atmosphere of a desert bazaar. Two department stores—"guarded" by pharaoh

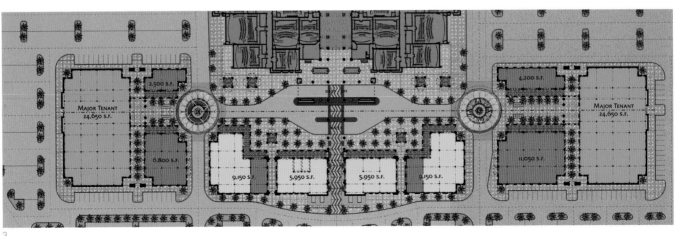

1

2

sculptures—anchor the ends of Paradise Park. Between them are a variety of specialty retail stores, boutiques, restaurants, and cafés, many accented with bright awnings. Alleyways between stores underscore the Egyptian bazaar theme, along with tent kiosks, water features, palms and other desert plants, Egyptian statuettes, sphinxes, obelisks, and columns covered with hieroglyphics. Parking is around the perimeter. Like its cinema namesake, Paradise Park gives meticulous attention to detail in theming to create a fun and inviting fantasy environment.

Imagery: 1   Retail view
           2   Cinema view along
               interior roadway
           3   Site plan

3

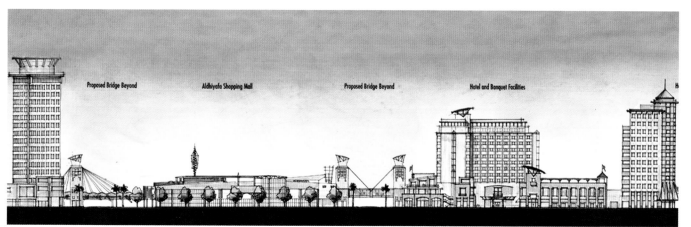

Aldhiyafa

Design/Completion: on-going
Makkah, Saudi Arabia
Aldhiyafa Real Estate Company, Ltd
Local architects: Schuster Pechtold &
Partners, UAE

Imagery: 1   Weekend bazaar
             2   Site plan
             3   Project elevation

The challenge to create a major retail master plan in the Saudi Arabian holy city of Makkah included integrating office, retail, hospitality, healthcare, and enhancing the identity of the existing mall and streetscape, while retaining the sanctity of the area.

Providing relief from the hot desert sun also posed a unique design challenge. The solution was to connect the various uses with a continuous retail arcade which wraps around a central shaded courtyard. This space is large enough to accommodate the traditional weekend bazaars, and interconnects with neighboring spaces, via tree-lined walks, creating a pedestrian-friendly street experience that is carried through the entire master plan.

The Aldhiyafa retail master plan succeeds in planning for the future by providing modern shopping, adaptable spaces for both modern and traditional uses, and reinforcing the identity of this cultural destination.

Proposed Bridge Beyond   Aldhiyafa Shopping Mall   Proposed Bridge Beyond   Hotel and Banquet Facilities

Warehouse Row

Design/Completion: 1988/1990
Chattanooga, Tennessee, USA
The Prime Group
300,000 square feet/27,881 square meters
Existing historic brick and timber structure
Brick, hardwood flooring, cast iron, plaster
and pre-cast concrete accents

Located in the heart of downtown Chattanooga, Warehouse Row creates a dynamic shopping and entertainment complex out of eight historic railroad warehouses built in the early 1900s. The two lower levels and basements have been transformed into a retail designer outlet mall, with major international retailers, boutiques, and cafés. Above are three levels of "Class A" office space. Designers retained the warehouse theme for the center, which both adds to its ambiance and helps it comply with strict Federal historic preservation regulations.

Storefronts in the retail mall were designed and pre-built, to ensure a consistent quality and character. Distressed wood floors reflect the warehouse theme. Two atrium skylights bring light into structures that nearly a century ago weren't built with light in mind. A system of ramps and steps has resolved inconsistencies of floor heights, and a distinctive staircase and elevator tower highlight the ease of transportation between levels. A footbridge connects the two main building areas on three levels. The bridge crosses over a ground-level pedestrian walkway which connects Warehouse Row to the surrounding neighborhood, linking at one end to Market Street and at the other to a fountain plaza and public park.

Warehouse Row has become a highly successful retail destination, regularly attracting visitors from as far away as Atlanta, 185 kilometers (115 miles) south.

ICSC Design and Development Award – Renovation/expansion of an existing project, Certificate of Merit, 1993

1

2

3

4

Imagery:
1   Interior mall
2   Basement food court
3   Urban park entry
4   Upper level
5   Ground floor plan

5

Festival Park

Design/Completion: 1999/under
construction
Palma de Mallorca, Spain
E.S. Mirall Development, S.A.
699,400 square feet/65,000 square meters
Reinforced concrete
Brick and stucco with ceramic and timber
accents, clay roof tiles

Two key design features help to re-organize and energize a central courtyard at the heart of this value retail and entertainment complex. One is Festival Park's landmark stair tower, with a wide stairway angling around it to the second level. The tower becomes something of an icon for the complex. The other is an aqueduct designed to resemble the arched Roman aqueducts common throughout southern Europe. The aqueduct forms a radius through the circular courtyard, and brings water into a pool and fountain at its center. An amphitheater encircles the pool, which can be fully or partially drained for performances. Courtyard kiosks, palm trees, and other landscaping also bring warmth and activity into the courtyard.

Another key feature is the forced perspective of Festival Park's main entry passageway. Its tapering shape draws visitors toward the central courtyard as they walk along a boutique-lined boulevard. A two-level restaurant promenade off the main plaza showcases a rhythm of structural arches at the ground level. Brightly colored umbrellas and outdoor seating enliven the first level; dining terraces above offer views of the activity below.

1

Imagery:

1	Central plaza
2	Main Street view
3	Site plan
4	View toward multiplex from Main Street
5	Above central plaza

2

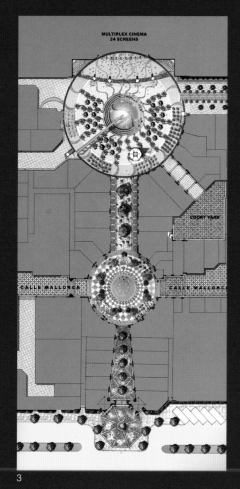

3

4

5

MUVICO PARADISE 24

BEACHSIDE ARUBA

DREAMLAND SHOPPING RESORT

UNICENTRO EL MARQUES

MENLYN PARK

MUVICO "DRIVE-IN"

MUVICO STARLIGHT 18

NEWPORT ON THE LEVEE

THE ZONE@ROSEBANK

STREETS OF MAYFAIR

TAI MALL

ENTERTAINMENT

Muvico "Paradise 24" Theater

Design/Completion: 1997/1999
Davie, Florida, USA
Muvico Theaters
100,000 square feet/9,300 square meters
Masonry bearing walls
Exterior finish insulation and GFRG (glass-fiber-reinforced gypsum)

Muvico "Paradise 24," one of Muvico Theaters' efforts to recreate the great movie palaces of the first half of the 20th century, reinvents the multiplex cinema as an Egyptian temple. The Egyptian theme begins beneath a porte-cochere supported by massive pharaonic columns. Neon column accents draw attention to the structure, and leaf motifs in the column capitals convey a sense of being in a forest of stone trees.

In the lobby, a glass mosaic "Nile River" snakes across a lotus-design floor carpet, directing moviegoers' movement through the complex. The river splits into tributaries at the "delta" of the concession area, which is flanked by pharaoh statues. Interior walls are distressed to convey the passage of time and covered with Egyptian-style paintings, murals, and hieroglyphics. The building is symmetrical, with 12 cinemas each in north and south wings extending from the main lobby. The north wing has cool Mediterranean blue tones, reflecting the fertility of Egypt's north. The golden carpet and multicolored sun design of the south wing evoke the sand, heat, and aridity of Egypt's south. Visitors enter the individual

theaters through entrances designed as portals into a temple. Inside, prominent graphic elements cover the sound panels. All theaters have stadium seating.

"Paradise 24" captures the theatrical aura of ancient Egypt as it helps restore the sense that going to the movies is an entertaining event. Its grandeur, attention to detail, and ethereal ambience create an atmosphere of magic and fantasy.

Muvico "Paradise 24" opened in March 1999 to record crowds and has shot to prominence as each weekend it ranks among the five highest-grossing theaters per capita in the United States.

Society of Environmental and Graphic Design, Juror's Award, 2000

Imagery:	1	Theater lobby
	2	Theater concessions
	3	Porte Cochiere
	4	Grand entry
	5	Auditorium
	6	Ground Floor Plan
Following pages		Paradise 24 at dusk

1

2

3

5

4

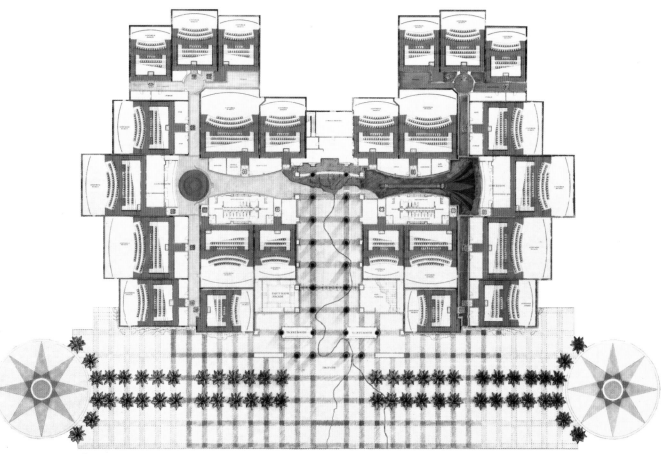

6

Beachside Aruba

Design/Completion: 1993/un-built
Aruba, Dutch Carribbean
Costa del Sol Developments
150,000 square feet/13,940 square meters
Reinforced concrete frame
Stucco, ceramic wall tile, clay tile roof

1

Part of a larger, master-planned resort community, Beachside Aruba is a design for a themed retail and entertainment resort village along Palm Beach, on the island's Caribbean coast. The architecture reveals strong Moorish and Moroccan influences, with its domes, arches, and whitewashed concrete walls designed to create a stark and striking contrast with the blue water of the sea. The three-level complex wraps around a central courtyard plaza marked by a saltwater pool, to be filled with moray eels,

manta rays, and other exotic tropical fish. Its "U" shape protects beach-goers from Aruba's notoriously strong easterly winds.

The complex, which includes restaurants, retail stores, a cinema, a casino, and other nightlife, is designed to become a retail and entertainment magnet for guests at the many hotels along this popular section of coastline. The design is sensitive to existing commerce, with an open-air market for local artisans, and an expansion of an existing fish market where Aruba's fishers sell their catch.

Beachside Aruba is not without a touch of irony. Its signature clock tower, which meshes nicely with the overall architectural theme, was inspired not by Moorish styles, but by the Bromo-Seltzer tower, a popular urban landmark that caught the client's eye when he saw it from Design Group's windows in the firm's home city of Baltimore, Maryland (USA).

2

Imagery:
1 Third-level courtyard view
2 Feature pavilion
3 View from marina
4 East/west section
5 Market entrance
6 Site plan

3

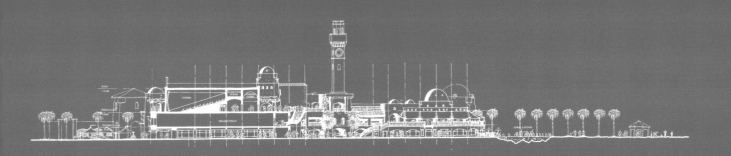

4

5

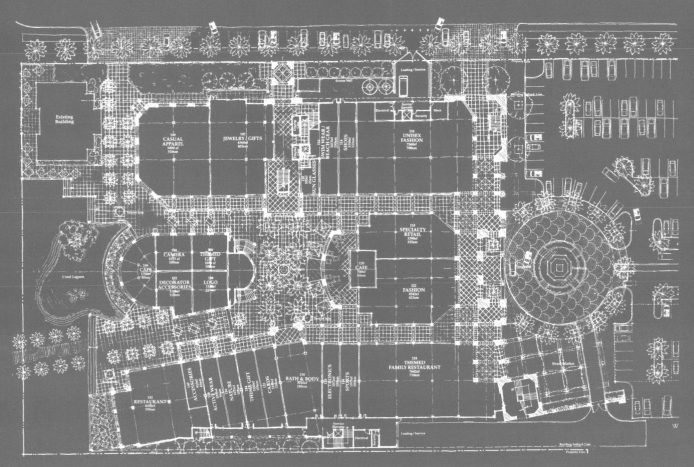

6

Dreamland Shopping Resort

Design/Completion: 1999/under construction
Cairo, Egypt
The Bahgat Group
Local architect: ASCG, Cairo
2,000,000 square feet/185,874 square meters
Reinforced concrete with brick and concrete
Plaster and stucco finish with faux stone, ceramic, metal and wood accents

Imagery:
1 Park Place elevation
2 Park Place under construction
3 Rotunda elevation
Opposite Concept model

The Dreamland Shopping Resort is the commercial and entertainment anchor of a larger, 930-hectare (2,300-acre) master planning effort that would create satellite cities to relieve some of the congestion around densely populated Cairo. (The Dreamland master plan is described in the Planning section, see page 164.) The shopping resort integrates the best of Old Cairo, with its narrow streets, mosques, and bazaars and waves of cultures and architectural styles, in a contemporary plan, with themed plazas and courtyards throughout its several "districts".

One district has a Mediterranean feel. A food court has an Islamic-inspired design. A children's play area is more contemporary. A cinema evokes an ancient Egyptian pharaoh's temple; a nearby market has the merchant tents and energy of the Grand Bazaar. A rotunda with its tile roof, concrete arches, and ornate brick-band accents picks up themes of Venice. Venice was also the inspiration for the canals running throughout the complex, which help create a sense of place for each district. Water for the canals is recycled and filtered from the nearby 6th of October City industrial complex.

In effect, the design takes a large retail and entertainment site and creates a small-scale shopping city, with themed designs influencing everything from major forms and passages to details such as rich-patterned floor paving, inverted flower umbrellas for shade, and the selection of materials. Construction on the center spine, linking the Grand Court, Grand Fountain, and Grand Rotunda, began in early 1999.

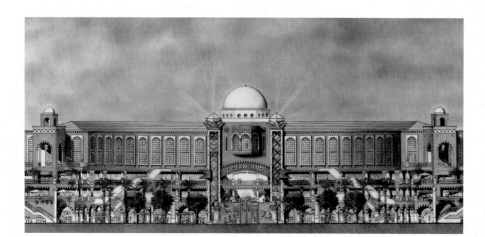

1

2

3

5

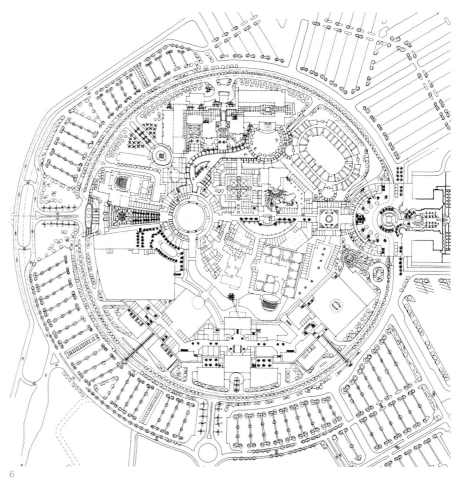

6

7

8

9

10

12

11

Imagery:

5	Phase 2 interior mall
6	Site plan (phase 2 lower half)
7	Entrance to phase 2
8	Canal Rotunda
9	Um-Kathume Court
10	Dancing waters
11	Aquarium entrance elevation to phase 2
12	The Bazaar

Unicentro El Marques

Current Project
Caracas, Venezuela
Grupo de Inversiones
Total: 753,200 square feet/70,000 square meters
Expansion: 29,052 square feet/2,700 square meters

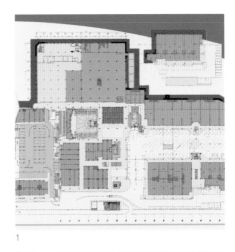

1

El Marques involves the renovation of an existing and popular shopping center built in the 1960s that is showing its age after nearly 40 years of use. The complex is on a major subway line and near a strong residential neighborhood, but is in need of an upgrade to remain competitive. The design for the complex integrates an anchor cinema (which will double in size from two screens to four), a children's play area, and many boutiques and restaurants. A food court with a major restaurant will be on one wing.

The original center was built in phases; one objective of the renovation is to unify the look. A chief way of accomplishing this will be to transform the façade, adding metal paneling, distinctive lighting, and powerful graphics, including large advertising panels that enhance the design while having the practical advantage of bringing in advertising revenue. New pylons and marquees will clarify entry points, orient visitors, and help connect El Marques to its surroundings. The design also adds an open, landscaped garden courtyard with a fountain and a performance stage.

The inside will also get a facelift. One important change will be to replace stark existing lighting—fluorescent bulbs suspended from a concrete ceiling—with a new drop ceiling and ambient lights, to add much-needed warmth and intimacy to the interior.

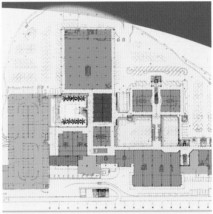

2

Imagery:

1 Avenida Fco. de Miranda level
2 Calle Arichuna level
3 Entertainment/food court level
4 North section elevation
5 View from Calle Arichuna
6 Proposed food court access section
7 Metro station/east wing cross section

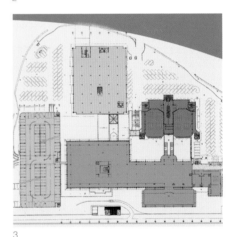

3

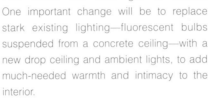

4

5

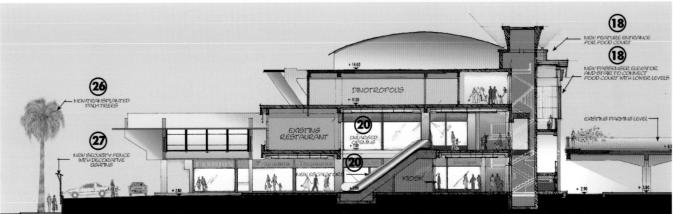

6

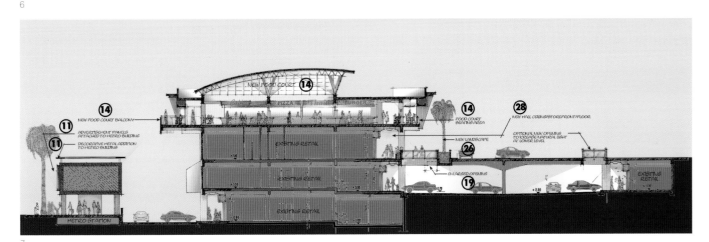

7

Menlyn Park

Design/Completion: 1997/2000
Pretoria, Republic of South Africa
Old Mutual Properties
Local architect: BILD Architects, Pretoria
1,200,000 square feet/111,524 square
meters
Reinforced concrete and steel structure with
steel roof and tension structure roof
Masonry back-up with stucco finish and
metal accents

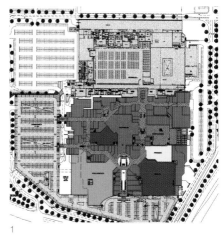

1

Although bigger often means more confusing, the renovation of Pretoria's Menlyn Park nearly doubled the size of this popular shopping center, while improving access and organization, and adding new feature spaces to increase its attractiveness to consumers. Working from a new master plan, Design Group expanded Menlyn Park vertically and horizontally, completing what were partial upper levels, and adding a new lower level to the east end. A new ring road enhances traffic circulation and provides entry into a six-level parking garage. Entry points have been simplified, and the new garage feeds directly into each of the center's three levels. The design imaginatively transforms the top level of the garage into a drive-in movie theater, which is adjacent to a 16-screen cinema.

Menlyn Park's most striking feature is the Grand Hall, a three-level court carved from the center of the complex. A tensile roof covers the hall, adding to its open and airy ambiance. Another innovation is Menlyn Events, an arena inspired by Roman amphitheaters that will provide a venue for activities ranging from rock concerts to soccer matches.

A new graphic identity, with colors and shapes inspired by traditional African patterns, complements design innovations throughout the center—which remained open during the renovation.

2

3

4

5

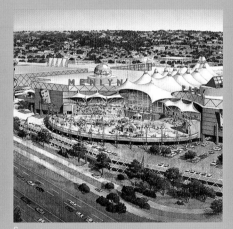

6

7

8

Muvico "Drive-In" Theater

Design/Completion: 1997/1998
Pompano Beach, Florida, USA
Muvico Theaters
86,000 square feet/7,990 square meters
Masonry bearing walls/steel frame
Exterior finish insulation and GFRG (Glass
Fiber Reinforced Gypsum)

Imagery: 1 Coffee bar
          2 Main concession
             stand

1

Muvico Pompano creates the illusion of going to a 1950s-style American drive-in movie theater. A black-top road with highway divider lines starts at the entrance and winds through the 18-screen complex, guiding visitors through a bold and graphically intense interior. Four antique cars over the entranceway, on a platform supported by telephone poles, project headlights toward a large tri-vision (drive-in) screen located above an art-deco concession area.

Two promenades extend off the central passageway. Marking the right wing is the Hot Spot Grill, with its large, sculpted coffee cup. On the left, a video arcade has the theme of a beachfront motel. Each wing has nine cinemas with stadium seating; each also has a satellite concession area. The red-and-white, checker-cloth tile design of the grill and the prominent red accent panels of the arcade/motel carry from the interior to the outside walls of the complex, merging with the peach and blue concrete of the surrounding sidewalk.

Since the 1950s drive-in used to be an after-dark destination, lighting is low, with powerful neon and graphic accents. The lobby floor is the dark blue of a lake at night, with star accents. In the ceiling, also dark blue, 10,000 blinking, fiber-optic stars create the illusion of mid-summer on a clear night.

2

1

Muvico "Starlight 20" Theater

Design/Completion: 1998/1999
Tampa, Florida, USA
Muvico Theaters
96,000 square feet/8,900 square meters
Masonry bearing walls/pre-cast concrete
double-tee roof
Exterior finish insulation and GFRG (Glass
Fiber Reinforced Gypsum)

The 1950s rural American diner provided the inspiration for Muvico Tampa Palms, and many design elements combine to create this effect. Moviegoers walk across pavement with a green-and-rose check tablecloth pattern to reach the box office. The box office is designed as a giant 1950s radio, and kiosks flanking it borrow their shape from diner jukeboxes. Behind the box office are seats that integrate tail fins of 1950s automobiles. A second-story, mock highway overpass winds along the walls through the interior, held up by telephone poles, with period trucks and cars along the raised roadway.

The centerpiece is the Hot Spot Diner, a 30-meter-wide (33-yard) concession area. A central crown, and neon light towers help break up the wide front, and are set against a night-sky backdrop accented with a red-check pattern. Imitation gas pumps are at each end.

A large barrel vault extends above the lobby, with the theater areas on two 10-screen wings extending to either side of the diner. A lobby video arcade with a motel theme anchors one wing; a children's play room the other. The playroom façade uses basic geometric shapes in bright primary colors, as though it had been built with oversized children's blocks. Bullnose stainless steel fronts with neon art-deco accents mark the theater entrances.

2

3

Newport on the Levee

Design/Completion: 1998/under
construction, 2001
Newport, Kentucky
Steiner & Associates
Local architect: GBBN Architects, Cincinnati
340,000 square feet/31,600 square meters
Reinforced concrete below grade, steel
frame above grade
Brick and exterior insulation system

1

Designed for a site next to an historic district on the Ohio River, Newport on the Levee continues the historical theme by creating a riverfront retail and entertainment complex for this Kentucky town. Located across the river from Cincinnati (Ohio), Newport adds an aquarium, an IMAX specialty theater, a 24-screen cinema, and a retail and entertainment mall with open-air and enclosed areas. A hotel and office complex are planned for the east end of the site. The project is a key component of a broader municipal effort to revitalize the greater Cincinnati region.

Visitors approaching the complex from an existing riverfront promenade climb a grand stairway to River Plaza, a circular entry plaza with a central fountain. To the west are the aquarium, whose design evokes a river barge, and the IMAX. To the east is the shopping mall and, above it, the cinema. The mall/cinema complex will be new, but designed in a gritty, aged style that gives it the look of a renovated Ohio River warehouse. Restaurants with outdoor seating overlook the promenade and the river. The tenant mix ranges from national retailers and entertainment companies to local jazz clubs.

Imagery:
1   Project aerial
2   Entry plaza
3   Interior atrium
4   Upper plaza
5   Aerial at entry plaza
6   Schematic sectional
    view facing north

2

3

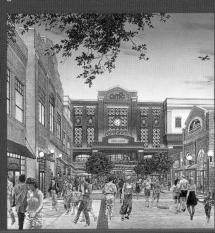
4

5

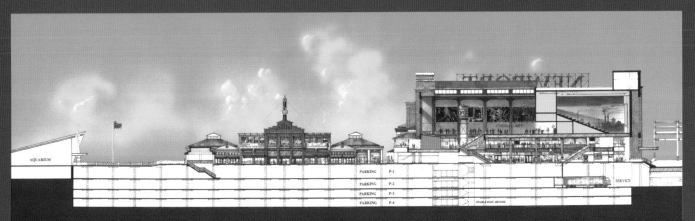
6

8

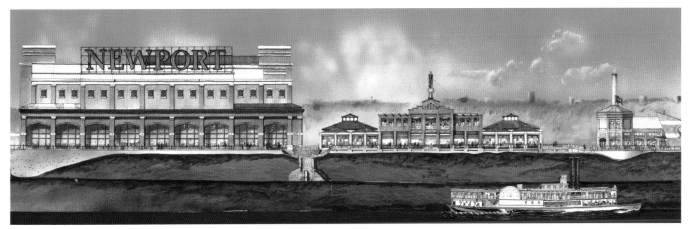

9

10

Imagery:
7   Drop-off court
8   Schematic east
     elevation at L&N
     Bridge
9   View of north
     façade from Ohio
     River
10   View of south façade
     from 3rd Street

The Zone@Rosebank

Design/Completion: 1998/2000
Johannesburg, Republic of South Africa
Old Mutual Properties
Local architect: LKA Architects,
Johannesburg
290,520 square feet/27,000 square meters
Waffle slab reinforced concrete, steel roof
Masonry back-up with stucco and metal
accents and aluminum panel system

Imagery: 1   View from Oxford
                       Road
               2   Study model at
                       Oxford and Tyrwhitt
                       Mall
       Opposite   Atrium cone

For all its visual intensity, two key features set the (loud) tone for the Zone@Rosebank, a bold, high-tech urban entertainment center in Johannesburg's inner suburb of Rosebank. One is the graphic power of an electrified streetscape, which takes advantage of Rosebank's enviable corner location at the intersection of Oxford Road, a major municipal artery, and Tyrwhitt Avenue, a popular pedestrian street. Rosebank engages the street, with the exterior chiefly serving as a medium for the contemporary graphic design expressions of its tenants, which include upscale boutiques, high-tech arcades, Internet cafés and themed restaurants, a department store, and a 14-screen multiplex cinema. Rather than leave these designs to chance, Design Group worked with tenants to ensure that their design identities were of a high-energy, studio-like quality. The studio environment also carries to interior mall and court areas, where tenants' merchandising and promotions take precedent.

The second defining feature is an imaginative, cone-shaped skylight that cuts through the center's core into the third-level lobby. An interior cylinder descends from the

1

cone through the first two levels, connecting the cinema lobby to the shopping area below. The dynamism of the cone shape and the rose-petal design of its skylight draw attention and movement upward. The cone walls at the cinema level double as projection screens for advertisements or movie trailers. At night, the shining cone is a beacon on the urban landscape.

2

4

5

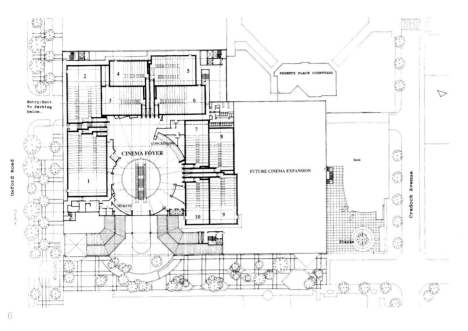

6

9

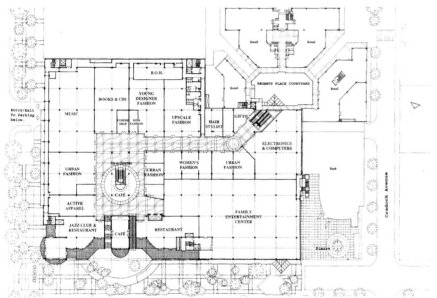

7

10

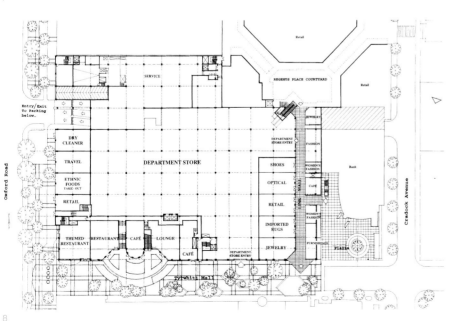

8

11

Streets of Mayfair

Design/Completion: 1993/1998
Miami, Florida, USA
Lennar Partners and Steiner & Associates
Local architect: Beame Architectural
Partnership
227,635 square feet/21,155 square meters
Existing reinforced concrete
Architectural concrete, stucco, plant
materials

In transforming the former Mayfair Shops in the Grove into the Streets of Mayfair, Design Group quite literally turned a struggling retail and entertainment center inside out. The former center was an imposing, inward-focused complex, with storefronts facing an interior courtyard, isolated from the neighborhood's surrounding streets and sidewalks. A confusing system of interior bridges and corridors blocked light and impeded navigation.

The renovation eliminated two of three interior courtyards and turned the complex outward toward the energy of Coconut Grove, a lively community west of Miami. A 40-foot-wide bridge was torn down to create the Promenade, a pedestrian street of boutiques, cafés, and outdoor entertainment that links the complex to the surrounding streets. Visitors have direct entry to the Promenade from a below-grade parking garage. Designers removed bridges and walkways to improve sight lines, and created a three-level galleria facing the street. The relocation of a 10-screen cinema to the third level creates a magnet that draws visitors through the center. A powerful new graphic identity, landscaping, neon lighting accents, and other features animate the streetscape and integrate it with the buildings. The restructured Streets of Mayfair is now a high-demand center of themed entertainment and shopping.

ICSC Design and Development Award – Certificate of Merit, Renovation/Expansion of an Existing Project, 1998

Imagery:

1   View from Grand
    Avenue
2   New Rice
    Street/plaza section
3   Cinema marquee
4   Plaza at Rice Street
5   New street façade

4

5

Tai Mall

Design/Completion: 1997/1999
Taipei, Taiwan R.O.C.
Tai Mall Development Company
1,631,540 square feet/151,630 square meters
Steel with reinforced concrete slab.
Teflon roof structure, copper roof
Stucco/exterior insulation system, GFRG (Glass Fiber Reinforced Gypsum), GFRC, porcelain tile, stain-pattern textured concrete

Imagery:
1   Castle gateway
2   Market gate
3   Mall level 6
4   Mall level 4
5   Mall level 2
6   Mall level 1

1

2

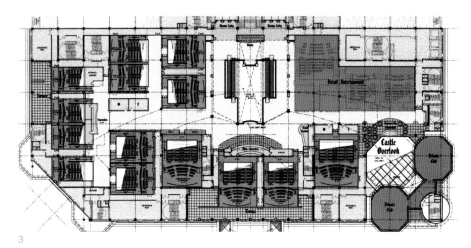

3

The huge box footprint and many structural parameters were in place when the developer approached Design Group to help create Tai Mall, a giant themed retail and entertainment complex in a suburb of Taipei. The developer wanted a castle theme for the complex, and previous attempts to create that theme had been too two-dimensional, amounting to little more than painting a castle on the side of a box. In contrast, Design Group added depth and relief to the façade, and brought the castle theme into the complex through imaginative corner turrets and a mid-street castle gate. Designers set these elements against an abstract, mountain-and-sky wall face, in green and indigo with a neon orange "sunset" accent line. These fantasy elements are part of a very serious effort to mitigate the scale of the existing massive building.

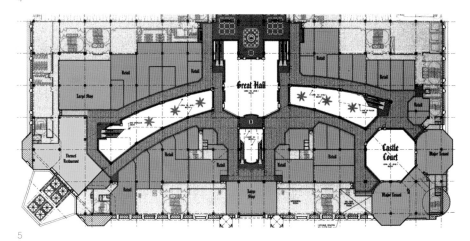

4

Throughout Tai Mall's seven levels are a variety of stores and boutiques, kiosks, restaurants and cafés, a food court, a hypermarket, and a 14-screen cinema complex. The mid-section has been carved out to create the mall's interior centerpiece: a great hall beneath an atrium skylight. The hall doubles as a performance stage, and can be viewed by visitors on all levels. Signature restaurants on different levels, a medieval banquet hall theme for the fourth-floor food court, a parking garage that feeds every level, and a seventh-floor cinema anchor promote vertical movement in the unusually tall complex.

ICSC Design and Development Award – Certificate of Merit, Innovative Design and Construction of a New Project, 2000

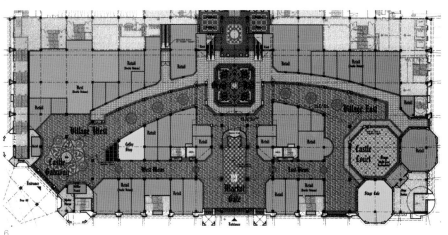

5

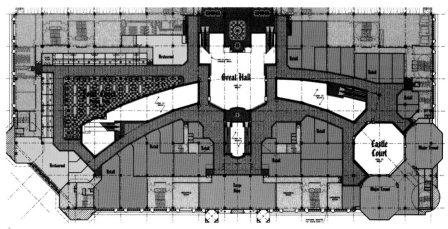

6

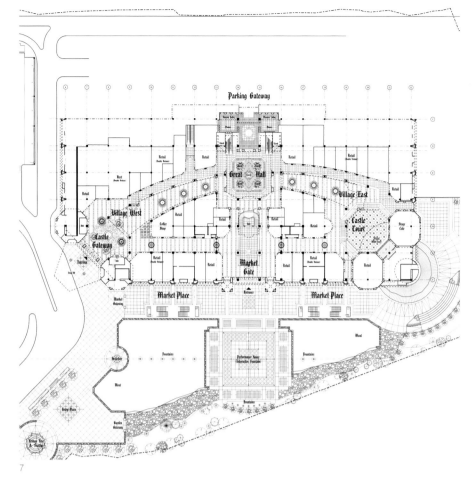

7

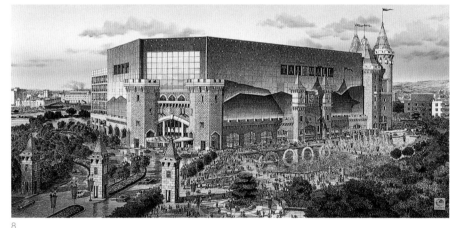

8

10

9

11

12

13

14

THE MARKETPLACE AT CASCADES

CORNELL TOWN CENTRE

EASTON TOWN CENTER

FAIRFAX CORNER

KENTLANDS RETAIL DEVELOPMENT

MERCHANTS SQUARE

LEGACY PLACE

TOWN CENTERS

Design/Completion: 1992/1994
Loudoun County, Virginia, USA
GFS Realty
213,660 square feet/19,857 square meters

Southbank Commons, a lively central block of stores and cafés, is the focal point of the Marketplace at Cascades Town Center, the commercial and community center of an affluent and growing suburb located west of Washington, DC. Stores with a range of façade designs and colors face tree-lined sidewalks with gas street lamps, banner graphics, and signage, creating an "old-town" main-street ambience. On-street parking improves access to Southbank Commons without impeding or threatening pedestrian movement.

Southbank Commons is a village hub connecting two open shopping areas. One is the Village Shops, anchored by a major supermarket and pharmacy. The other is the Shops at Park Place, linked to the commons by a new city park. Designers worked within the constraints of a traditional street-grid plan to create a hybrid development equally suited to the needs of small businesses and large retailers accustomed to open-center locations.

Cascades Marketplace is the shopping and entertainment center of a 42-hectare (105-acre), master-planned community.

It integrates the warmth and smaller scale of American town centers from an earlier era with the parking and access demands of contemporary retailers.

ICSC Innovative Design of a New Project, Certificate of Merit, 1996

Imagery:

1	Site plan
2	Main streetscape
3	Town center
4	Streetscape
5	Entry signage
6	View from Park Place

4

5

6

7

8

9

10

11

Cornell Town Centre Master Plan

Design/Completion: 1997/on-going
Markham, Ontario, Canada
Law Development Group
Total land area: 250 acres/101 hectares
Gross building area: 6,624,716 square feet/
615,680 square meters

1

The centerpiece of this town center master plan for a new community, located in Markham, Ontario, near Toronto, is an 8-hectare (20-acre), artificial lake that will both attract the interest of passersby on the new ring road around Toronto, and provide a buffer between community residents and the highway. The lake itself is designed for sailing and other water sports, and a lakefront promenade is a place of high activity, with a semi-circular entertainment pavilion, and numerous shops and restaurants along its length.

Cornell Town Centre integrates commercial, retail, entertainment, office, and residential sectors in a vibrant town core. The village center and main residential area is Main Street Cornell, to the north, with townhouses, residential towers, and retail shops oriented around a central plaza and fountain. A hotel anchors the northern end of Main Street, and many offices and living/work accommodations serve an adjacent medical center.

Main Street crosses Highway 7, and connects to Cornell Crescent, the lakefront entertainment district. To the west are a

sports complex (with eight ice hockey rinks), a cinema, community center, apartments, and a hotel, conference, and exhibition center. To the east is a park that preserves existing woodlands, and east of that, an office complex, with a Cyber Park suited to the region's growing high-tech industry.

Mid-block parking, buildings positioned on property lines, and pedestrian-friendly streets with pedestrian access to town-center amenities are among the tenets of New Urbanism found in the Cornell Town Centre master plan.

Imagery:
1   Charrette in Toronto
2   Model of crescent
3   Early concept model
4   Master plan
5   Waterfront
     promenade

2

3

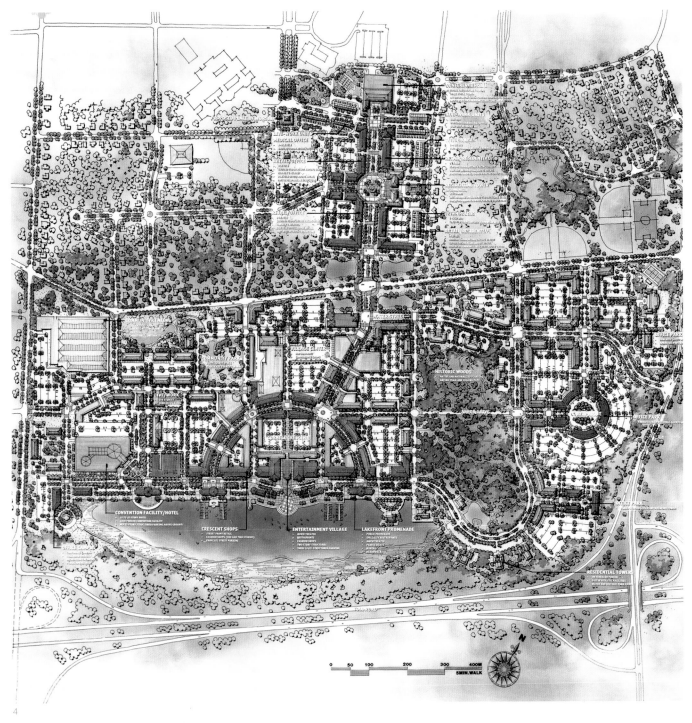

CONVENTION FACILITY/HOTEL
- 18 TO 20 STORY HOTEL
- 4,000 PERSON CONVENTION FACILITY
- MULTI-STORY STRUCTURED PARKING ABOVE GROUND

CRESCENT SHOPS
- STREET FRONT RETAIL
- FASHION SHOPS (ONE AND TWO STORIES)
- PARKLESS STREET PARKING

ENTERTAINMENT VILLAGE
- MOVIE THEATER
- RESTAURANTS
- FASHION SHOPS
- TWO STORY STRUCTURES
- THREE LEVEL STRUCTURED PARKING

LAKEFRONT PROMENADE
- PUBLIC PROMENADE
- SPECIALTY SYSTEM UNITS
- AMPHITHEATRE
- PADDLE BOATS
- MARINAS
- BOARDWALKS

0   50   100   200   300   400M
5 MIN. WALK

4

5

Easton Town Center

Design/Completion: 1995/1999
Columbus, Ohio, USA
Georgetown Ltd/Steiner + Associates
Consultant: Rockwell Group (AMC Theaters)
Phase I GLA: 650,000 square feet/60,409 square meters
Phase II GLA: 750,000 square feet/69,703 square meters

Imagery:
1   "Train shed" gallery
2   Gallery storefronts
Opposite   Gallery entry plaza

An antidote to suburban sprawl, Easton Town Center is a mixed-use town center with a mid-America theme that integrates shopping with entertainment, recreation, office space, and other public amenities. Easton adapts the New Urbanism school of town design in ways that reflect its setting near the city of Columbus.

Designers used storyboards to plan Easton, adapting vernacular themes of Midwestern American towns in the first half of the 20th century to contemporary uses. A major bookstore is designed as a library, a fitness center looks like a high school gym, and a fire station has been reincarnated as a bakery. Easton's centerpiece is an enclosed mall designed as a traditional Midwestern train station, with a 30-screen cinema, high-tech video arcade, and other entertainment-oriented tenants. Smaller stores and cafés at street level fill out Easton's rigid street grid. Office space is above the stores on the second level. Narrow streets and on-street parking slow cars traveling through town, keeping wide sidewalks safe for pedestrians. Design themes from a range of eras create variety and a sense of a town that has evolved naturally over time.

2

Easton Town Center is the first phase of a larger plan that calls for additional office and commercial space, residential neighborhoods, parks, and other features radiating out from the town center. Phase two is expected to add nearly 70,000 square meters (750,000 square feet) of leasable space.

ICSC Design and Development Award – Design Award, Innovative Design and Construction of a New Project, 2000

1

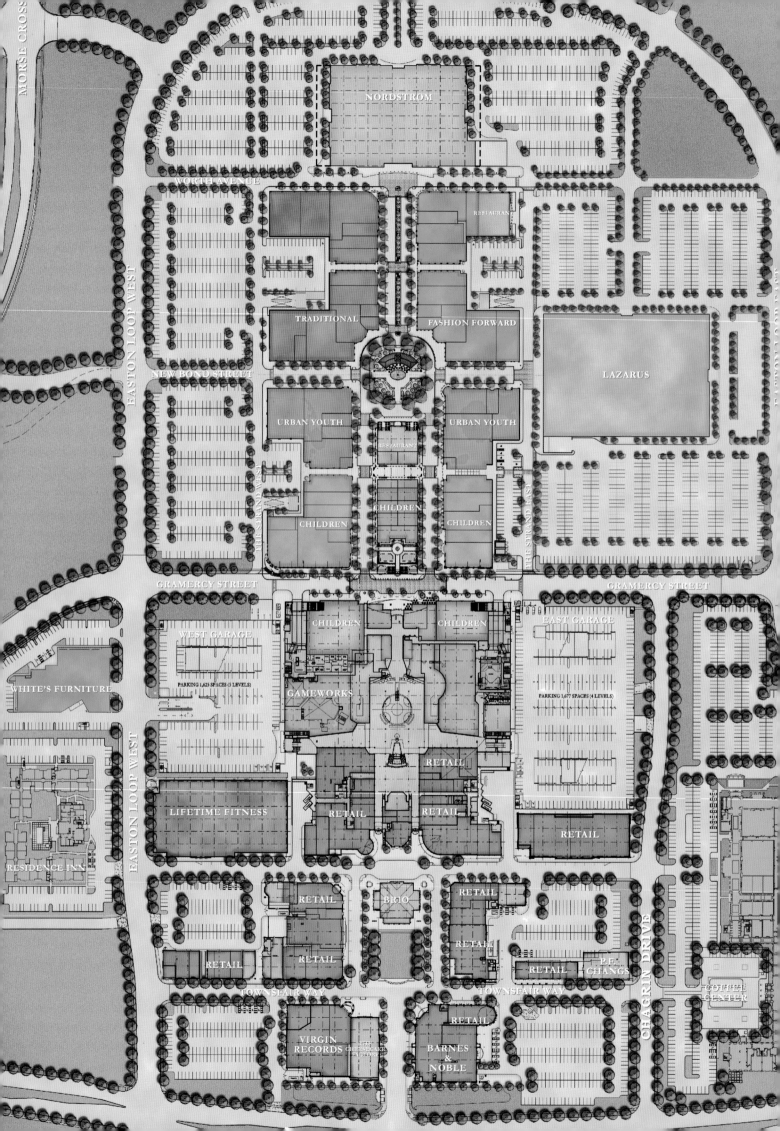

6

7

5

8

9

10

11

12

13

14

Imagery: 11 Pop fountain
12&14 Town square events
13 Sorority initiation
Below Town square

16

17

18

19

Fairfax Corner

Current project
Fairfax, Virginia, USA
The Peterson Companies
480,000 square feet/44,610 square meters

1

Fairfax adapts the neo-traditional town-center master plan concept to a larger, urban-scale grid in a growing suburb west of Washington, DC. The developer sought to adapt what he saw and liked at Easton Town Center (see page 88) to a more urban and cosmopolitan community.

The central anchor of the plan is a multi-screen cinema complex, with a fountain plaza and an open-air promenade running perpendicular to Kings Way, the community's main street. Retail stores and restaurants line the promenade. South of the cinema is the town commons, flanked by office buildings with stores at the ground level. Fairfax's main residential section is north of the cinema.

Fairfax takes advantage of growth plans for the Washington metropolitan area. Office parks are springing up along the Interstate 66, west of the city, creating a need for new "edge cities" along that highway corridor. The region immediately surrounding Fairfax is zoned residential, and a new subway extension will soon reach its doorstep.

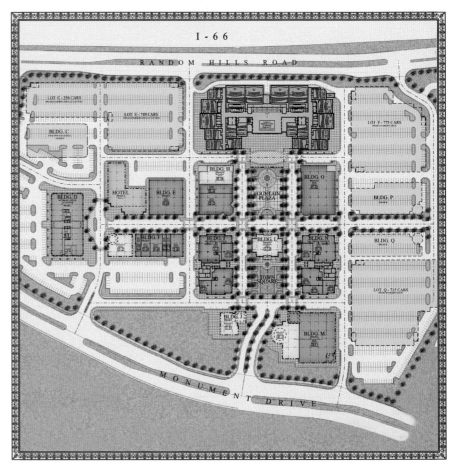

2

3

4

5

6

Kentlands Retail Development

Design/Completion: 1991/1999
Gaithersburg, Maryland, USA
Beatty Companies/Great Seneca
Development Company
525,000 square feet/48,792 square meters
Steel frame
Brick and stucco with metal accents

Kentlands, near Washington, DC, was one of the earliest neo-traditional town plans developed by Andres Duany and Elizabeth Plater-Zyberk, pioneers of the New Urbanism school of community development. Design Group was asked to develop a creative plan for a retail center anchored by a supermarket, a major hardware and home products store, and a leading budget retailer.

Designers adapted the town plan of city blocks in a traditional grid layout to the power center, using a grid, along with trees and other landscaping, to break up large parking areas into their own separate "blocks". This reduced the massiveness of what in traditional strip centers is typically a large, disorienting asphalt field, while reflecting the character and scale of the town of Kentlands. The monumental pediment façades and white colonnades of the stores also pick up on the town's classical American themes.

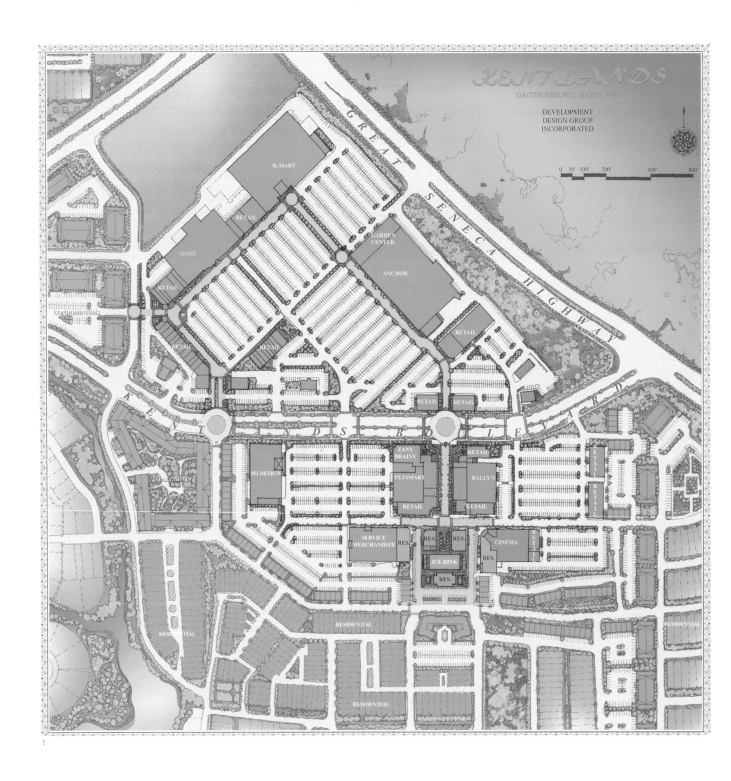

1

A second phase of the Kentlands project created Market Square, a smaller scale, pedestrian-friendly street in the same classical American-town style, with shops, restaurants, a cinema, an ice rink, and a city park.

2

3

5

4

Imagery:

1 Master plan
2 View from Great Seneca Highway entrance
3 Entry signage
4 View from Kentlands Boulevard
5 Market Square concept model

Merchants Square

Current project
Williamsburg, Virginia, USA
The Colonial Williamsburg Foundation
386,250 square feet/35,896 square meters
Existing historic structures, steel frame
Traditional brick and wood clapboard

1

Merchants Square involves rejuvenating and doubling the size of the retail and entertainment district in Colonial Williamsburg, a popular tourist destination noted for historical accuracy in restoring a social and cultural center of 17th and 18th century America. The design challenge is to invigorate Merchants Square in ways that help it remain competitive with the many theme parks and outlet malls in this growing area, while remaining consistent with the town's historic character.

Shops and restaurants line both sides of Duke of Gloucester Street, a pedestrian street that extends from the campus of the College of William and Mary, east into the town's restored colonial sector. The design calls for the addition of buildings around existing parking courts, and variety in building façades, to reflect the historic urban character of a town that evolved building-by-building during the colonial era. Street-level passageways between buildings will reinforce this effect, and will draw visitors to businesses beyond the main street. A new, four-level parking garage will be mostly

below grade, to avoid the visual abruptness commonly associated with structures of this size and type. A multi-screen cinema complex is also planned.

The merchandising mix integrates national and international retailers with regional and local merchants. New stores have been selected for the double benefit of attracting tourist shoppers, and reconnecting the square with students attending William and Mary College. The relocation of the college bookstore to a former department store in the square will support this integration.

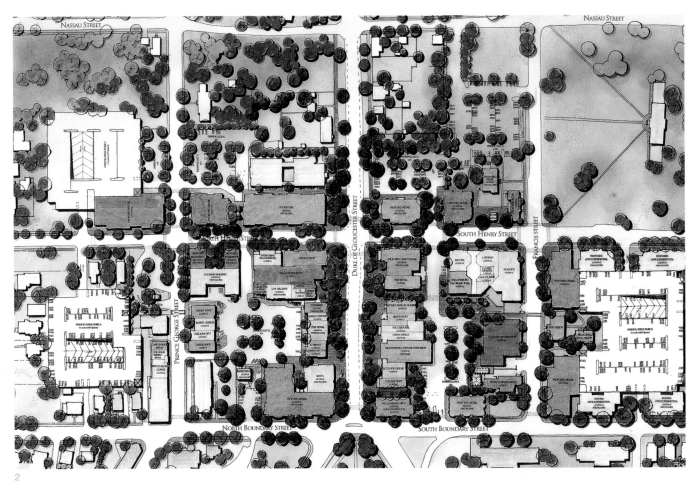

2

3

Imagery:

1   Existing streetscape
2   Site plan
3   View from Duke of
      Gloucester Street
4   South elevation
5   West elevation

RETAIL TENANT-1   BINNS' EXPANSION   BINNS' EXISTING SHOP

BUILDING A

4

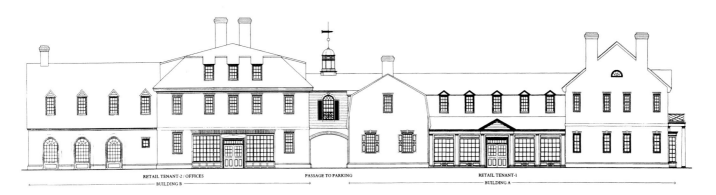

RETAIL TENANT-2 / OFFICES   PASSAGE TO PARKING   RETAIL TENANT-1

BUILDING B   BUILDING A

5

Legacy Place

Current project
Palm Beach, Florida, USA
Catalfumo Construction & Development,
Inc.
Local architect: Oliver & Glidden
Partnership, West Palm Beach, Florida
467,330 square feet/43,432 square meters
Steel frame
Exterior insulation system, pre-cast plaster
trim

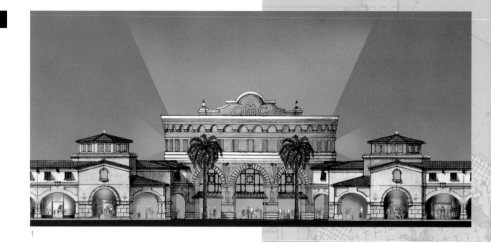
1

The use of angles in the plan for Legacy Place, the design for a town center in Palm Beach Gardens, Florida, adds variety to a central promenade, promoting movement in ways that could not be achieved with a more standard, linear approach. The central Mizner Loop courtyard (so called because it was inspired by the prototype Mizner Park in nearby Boca Raton) doglegs at one end to one anchor, a major bookseller. At the opposite end, another anchor – a multi-screen cinema complex – is likewise skewed off the central axis, with a massive drum entrance as its pivot point. These subtle twists prevent long views from one end of Legacy Place to the other, adding a sense of allure and discovery to draw visitors along the length of the complex. Colorful fabric canopies and Mediterranean style arcades along the street provide continuous cover for visitors. At night, façade and landscape lighting, and accent lights cast skyward from the cinema drum attract drivers passing by on an adjacent highway.

Legacy Place is a true mixed-use center, with stores and restaurants at ground level, and residences and office space above.

2

Imagery:
1 Cinema Elevation
2 Grand Avenue
3 Restaurant court
4 Site plan
5 Aerial
6 Valet-serviced arrival Court
7 Overall project view

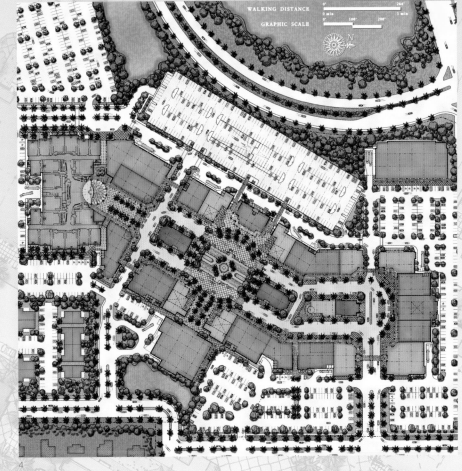

WALKING DISTANCE

GRAPHIC SCALE

N

3

4

5

6

7

COLONIAL PLAZA

BALTIMORE INTERNATIONAL YACHTING CENTER

CITRALAND GROGOL

PALMERA

DHARMALA ALDIRON

YUAN HONG CITY

ROBERTSON WALK

SENOPATI

KEBON MELATI

MIXED USE

Colonial Plaza

Design/Completion: 1998/under construction
Caracas, Venezuela
Grupo de Inversiones
664,140 square feet/61,700 square meters
Concrete frame
Stucco, precast concrete, timber, ceramic
tile, cobblestone pavers, ornamental iron

The design for Colonial Plaza takes advantage of the topography of Caracas to create a multi-tiered hill town in the 17th-century Spanish Colonial vernacular architecture of South America. The retail–entertainment complex is actually three distinct plazas at different elevations, connected by a pedestrian street surrounded by arcades.

Center Plaza, with a palm-tree-lined open-air courtyard, a 13-screen cinema, an events stage, and many small shops and restaurants, is the heart of the complex. The street at one end leads up 10-meter-wide Spanish-style steps to the East Plaza, which features a child-oriented family entertainment area and fountain for children's play, and bell-towers reminiscent of Spanish Colonial churches. Between the Center and East Plazas is an open-air market in a warehouse-like building supported by timber trusses. The market is filled with kiosks, creating the atmosphere of a European bazaar. At Center Plaza's other end, steps lead down to the more quiet and secluded West Plaza, whose structures evoke early municipal buildings in the region. A nine-story office complex is also at this end.

Stucco, tile, and marble accents reinforce the overall theme and suit the tropical Venezuelan climate. Construction on Colonial Plaza began in 2000.

Imagery: below Market building
section
2 East Plaza level plan
3 Center Plaza level
plan
4 West Plaza level
plan
5 Ground level plan

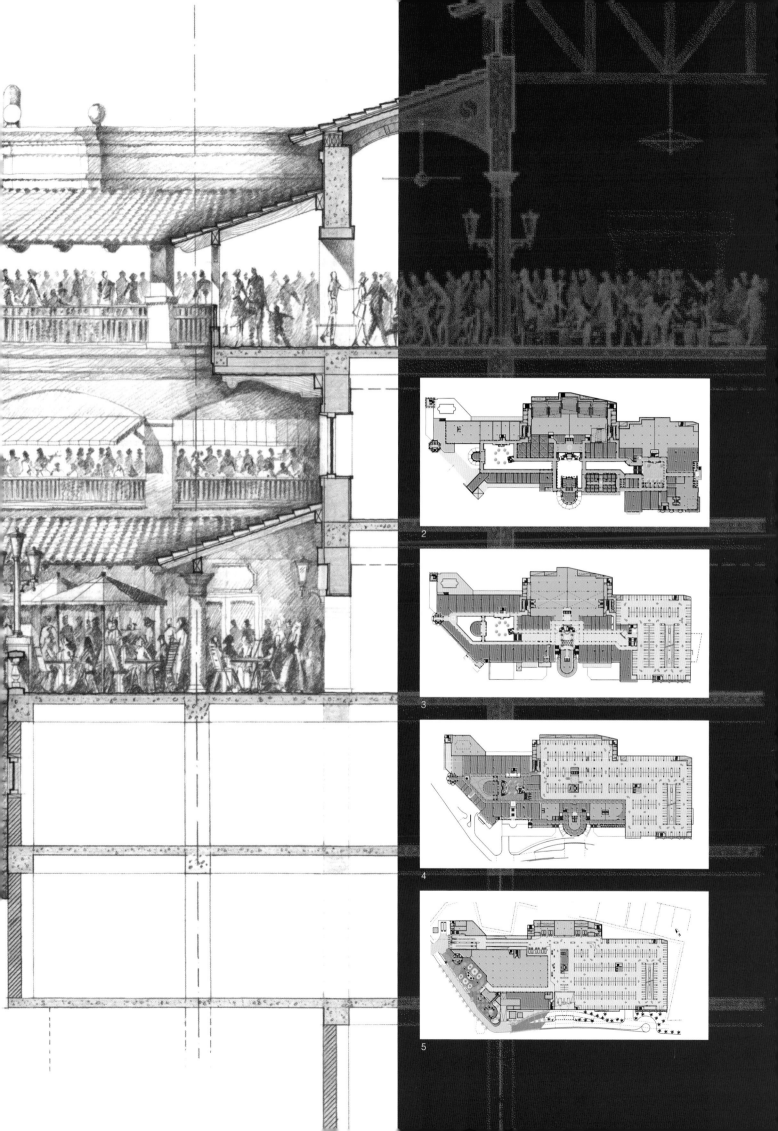

2

3

4

5

7

8

9

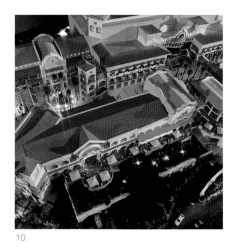

10

11

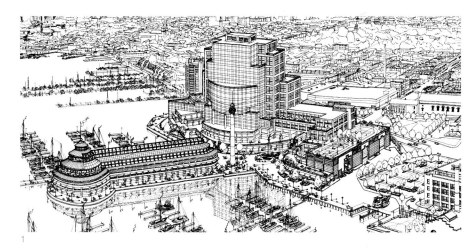

The Baltimore International Yachting Center

Design/Completion: 1992/un-built
Baltimore, Maryland, USA
Marina Ventures, Inc.
700,000 square feet/65,056 square meters

1

The design for the Baltimore International Yachting Center sought to create a waterfront landmark to anchor development in the eastern part of the city, while also becoming a showcase yachting destination for the country. Baltimore Harbor, at the northern end of the Chesapeake Bay, was an ideal location for the center, a multi-use complex with nautical-theme businesses, a hotel, and residential and office space.

The design removed two existing piers to build its signature retail and commercial pier. It has a skylit atrium promenade leading to a

tiered, circular structure that takes its shape from a traditional lighthouse design common throughout the Bay area. The promenade has restaurants and a variety of marine retailers, and passes through a grand boat hall where boat merchants can show off their latest designs. An L-shaped hotel opens onto the pier; a "boatel" yacht storage facility is next to and under the hotel.

On land, the nautical theme carries into the tower. A yacht club at its base also adopts the Bay lighthouse shape, while above the yacht club the building juts toward the water

like a ship's prow. Throughout the center, shapes mimic natural and human-made maritime forms, and bright colors in the buildings and graphics are the same as those found in yachting clothes, gear, and flags.

2

3

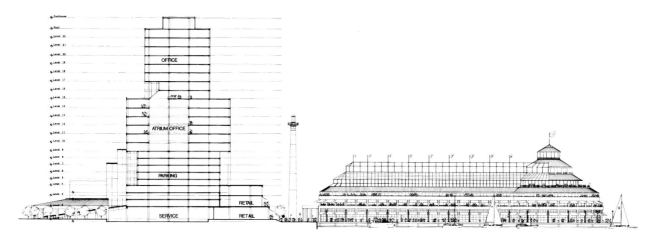

4

Imagery: 1 Aerial perspective
          2 Marina view
          3 Building form
          4 Project section
          5 Boat hall
          6 Site plan

5

6

Citraland Grogol

Design/Completion: 1990/1992
Jakarta, Republic of Indonesia
PT Citra Niaga Plaza
Local architect: PT Perentjana Djaja
1,000,680 square feet/93,000 square meters
Reinforced concrete frame
Masonry with plaster façade, pre-cast
plaster accents, glass skylights and curtain
wall system

Imagery:
1 Ramped walkways
2 Exterior view
3 Project section
4 Upper mall
5 Upper ground-floor plan
6 Fourth-level plan
7 Atrium bridges

1

Citraland uses an intriguing and ambitious design to promote movement through an exceptionally tall, nine-level shopping complex. Four key factors contribute to the success of the design. First is the placement of a destination food court and multi-screen cinema on the upper levels, which encourages movement upward. Second, the multi-use complex provides direct connections to the mall from the adjacent Hotel Ciputra, a wedge-shaped structure that towers over and sits inside the "L" of the mall. Third, the parking garage is six levels tall, and enhances access by feeding directly into the mall at each level.

The final and most ingenious factor stimulating vertical movement is an almost Escher-like, ramped circulation scheme that moves visitors up or down one level as they travel from one end of the mall to the other. The neon-accented ramps have become an attraction of their own, adding an element of surprise to movement within the mall.

The "L" shape is oriented to take advantage of an enviable location on the main highway to the Jakarta airport. Strong lighting and graphic elements – such as neon-accented roof arches on the hotel wings that pick up the design of an atrium arch in the mall's center, and a tower beacon at the elbow of the hotel – engage travelers arriving in Jakarta.

Pacific Coast Builders Conference Gold Nugget Award – Merit Award, Best Commercial Retail, 1994

2

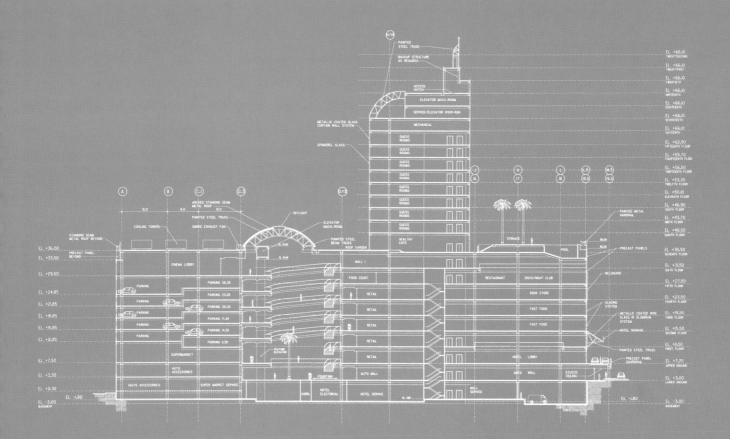

3

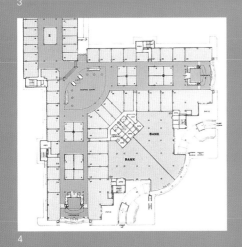

4

5

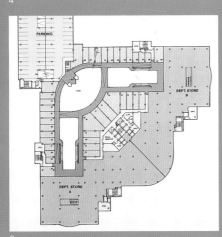

6

7

Palmera

Design/Completion: 1997/un-built
Cairo, Egypt
Omar Al-Mutawa/ECG/National Contracts Group
4,304,000 square feet/400,000 square meters
Concrete frame with steel trusses
Masonry, stucco curtainwall, stone, metal, pre-cast concrete accents

atrium rotunda highlights the entertainment center's main interior courtyard, and streets with Mediterranean and African themes branch off from it.

Imagery:

1 Entry court
2 Site plan
3 Office park
4 Mall view
5 Water park
6 Center court
7 Themed mall
8 Ice rink
9 Airport access road

An unusual aspect of the design for Palmera is the attention designers gave to how it would look from the air. Designed for a narrow, sloping site adjacent to the Cairo airport, the L-shaped complex effectively becomes an aerial-view, welcome-to-Egypt poster for the 20 million travelers who fly over it every year. The ibis, the Great Eye, the scarab, and other identifiable Egyptian motifs have been integrated into building designs, water features, and the landscape. These culturally significant images are especially appropriate, given that Palmera is located in Heliopolis, a planned city named for an important ancient center of culture and worship.

Palmera is designed for tourists and travelers, as well as for the residents of Heliopolis, with a power center of large specialty retailers and smaller stores, an office complex, a country club, and a luxury hotel, whose scarab-shaped pool and a sundial at its entrance are signature landmarks. Retail centers flank a central entertainment complex, with attractions ranging from high-tech, interactive arcades and a 10-screen cinema to a bowling alley, an ice rink, and a climbing wall. A skylit

1

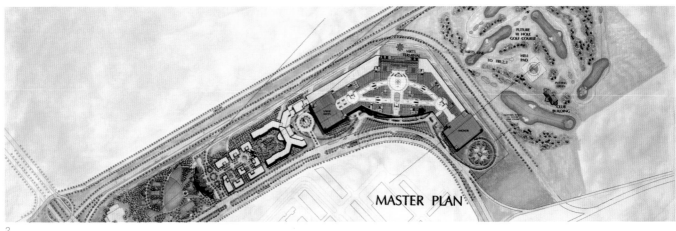

MASTER PLAN

2

3

4

5

6

7

8

9

Dharmala Aldiron

Design/Completion: 1994/unbuilt
Jakarta, Republic of Indonesia
PT Dharmala Intiland
559,520 square feet/52,000 square meters
Cast-in-place concrete
Curtainwall aluminum frame windows, stone
and metal cladding

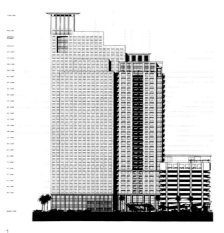

1

Imagery: 1   North elevation
         2   West elevation
         3   South elevation
         4   Site plan
Opposite   East elevation

2

3

The main challenge in developing the design for Dharmala Aldiron, a planned 30-story, mixed-use complex in downtown Jakarta, was to combine as many square meters of residential and office space as possible on a very tight, 1.3-hectare site. A related challenge was creating separate office and residential towers. The solution was to connect the towers and to give them distinct, yet aesthetically complementary identities.

The fenestration creates the most marked visual distinction between the towers. The larger windows and modern curtainwall of the office tower are well suited to business uses. In contrast, the smaller inset windows of the residential tower create a more intimate effect, adding privacy and helping to reduce both noise and heat. In order to visually unite the designs, the vertical massing and architectural detailing of each tower reflect the façade elements of the other. Tiered towers and corner stepping help to mitigate the mass of the structure while increasing the number of corner rooms and penthouse apartments. To reinforce the separate tower identities, the office entrance along a main street is the grander of the two; the residential entrance is more intimate, and off the main road. A smaller, attached structure serving both towers provides such amenities as parking, a market, a fitness center, tennis courts, and a rooftop pool.

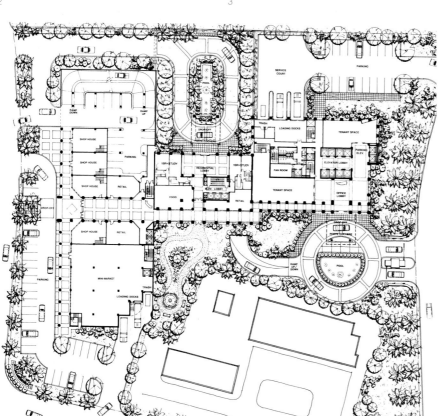

4

Yuan Hong City

Design/Completion: 1992/partially complete 2000, on-going
Fuzhou, People's Republic of China
Salim Group
4,411,600 square feet/410,000 square meters
Reinforced concrete
Concrete block with ceramic tile

The nine towers of Yuan Hong City, a design for a site in Fuzhou, on the Min River in southeastern China, show the influence of the Chinese art of Feng Shui on Design Group's work. The positioning of the buildings with respect to water and other elements, the pointed rooftop towers, and even the number nine, reflect tenets of this ancient art of creating and arranging environments.

Five residential towers on one side and a single hotel tower on the other flank the taller towers of a central office and retail complex. The residential towers and hotel are oriented toward the river and a public riverside park. Between the hotel and office complex is an upscale shopping center, which was the first part of Yuan Hong to be built, opening in 2000. The master plan called for the towers to be built, sold, and financed individually.

The office/retail complex is oriented away from the river toward an urban shopping district. A glass-roofed atrium arches above a retail and entertainment center at the base of the office towers. The atrium opens at ground level onto an outdoor office plaza that links the complex to the shopping district.

1

2

Distinctive light towers at either side of the atrium become beacons at night, and neon storefront graphics also enliven the streetscape.

Imagery:
1 Riverfront towers
2 View from Tai Jiang road
3 Winter garden atrium
4 Site plan
5 View from Min River

3

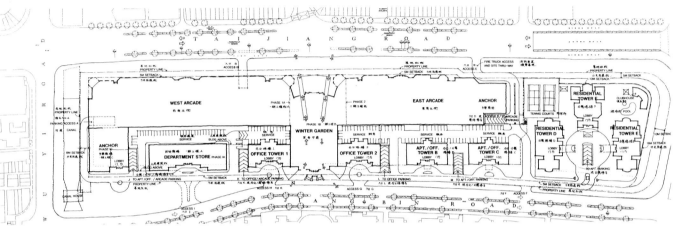

4

5

Robertson Walk

Design/Completion: 1995/1997
Singapore
Centre Point Properties, Ltd
314,127 square feet/29,194 square meters
Reinforced concrete
Stone, stucco, pre-cast concrete and
mosaic tiles

Imagery: 1   Plaza at dusk
             2   Early concept sketch
             3   Fountain plaza   1

2

Though its two residential towers are ten stories high, several design features help give this mixed-use development near the Singapore River a human scale, and orient it toward the street. The two-story retail-and-entertainment base adapts an indigenous Chinese "shop house" style of architecture, with second-floor façades designed to look as though they were the dwellings of shop owners. A covered exterior walkway and tile-roof overhang reinforce this effect, as do window treatments ranging from Bahama shutters and French-door style shutters, to colorful canvas awnings.

A major focal point for Robertson Walk is a central, open-air courtyard, with cobblestone paving, colorful flags, push-cart merchants, and rich landscaping. Ground-level restaurants and cafés engage both the courtyard and the surrounding street. Another focal point is the river itself, connected to Robertson Walk by a pedestrian walkway marked with strong graphics and signage.

The towers, one a 90-unit apartment building and the other a 90-unit condominium complex, are stepped back from the retail base, and are tiered to reduce the impact of their height. Façade and window treatments pick up on the "shop house" theme. Red tile roofs, pastel tones, wrought iron railings, and stucco and stone façades with hand-painted terra cotta tile inlays reinforce the village-courtyard ambiance. Residents can take advantage of such amenities as a rooftop garden, clubhouse, pool, and recreation and sports facilities.

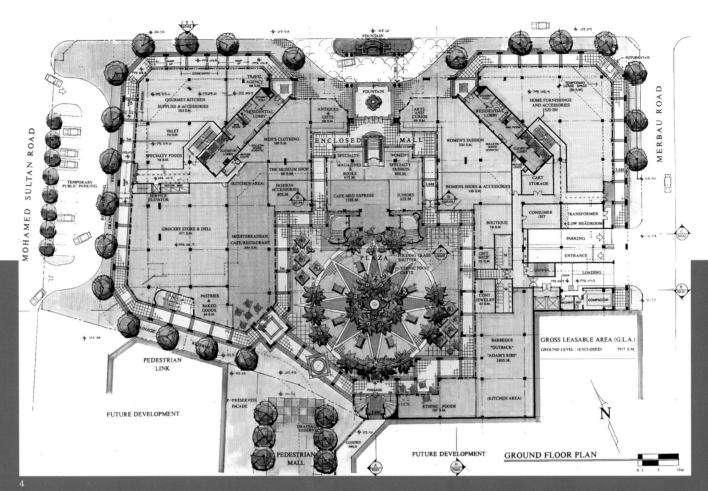

FOUNTAIN

FOUNTAIN

TRAVEL AGENCY 88 S.M.

GOURMET KITCHEN SUPPLIES & ACCESSORIES 263 S.M.

RESIDENTIAL LOBBY

ANTIQUES & GIFTS 68 S.M.

ARTS AND CURIOS 66 S.M.

HOME FURNISHINGS AND ACCESSORIES 520 SM

RESIDENTIAL LOBBY

TEMPORARY LEASE SPACE 38 S.M.

FUTURE STAIR

VALET 70 S.M.

ELEVATOR LOBBY

MEN'S CLOTHING 186 S.M.

ENCLOSED MALL

ESCALATORS

WOMEN'S FASHION 233 S.M.

SPECIALTY FOODS 78 S.M.

SPECIALTY

WOMEN'S SPECIALTY FASHION 80 S.M.

CART STORAGE

THE MUSEUM SHOP 40 S.M.

MAGAZINES & BOOKS 65 S.M.

TEMPORARY PUBLIC PARKING

FASHION ACCESSORIES 80 S.M.

SERVICE ELEVATOR

CAFE MED EXPRESS 158 S.M.

JUNIORS 62 S.M.

WOMENS SHOES & ACCESSORIES 149 S.M.

CONSUMER /HT

TRANSFORMER 4.2 LOW HEADROOM

GROCERY STORE & DELI 571 S.M.

MEDITERRANEAN CAFE/RESTAURANT 394 S.M.

BOUTIQUE 78 S.M.

PARKING

PLAZA

FOLDING GLASS SHUTTER

ETHNIC FOOD CARTS

GIFT SHOP 25 S.M.

ENTRANCE

LOADING

PASTRIES & BAKED GOODS 84 S.M.

RESERVE

CONT. JEWELRY 40 S.M.

SECURITY POST

COMPACTOR

PEDESTRIAN LINK

PRESERVED FACADE

DRAINAGE RESERVE

BARBEQUE "OUTBACK" "ADAM'S RIBS" 380 S.M.

GROSS LEASABLE AREA (G.L.A.)

GROUND LEVEL : (ENCLOSED)   3917 S.M.

FUTURE DEVELOPMENT

PASSAGE

COVERED WALK

(KITCHEN AREA)

ETHNIC FOODS 137 S.M.

PEDESTRIAN MALL

FUTURE DEVELOPMENT

N

GROUND FLOOR PLAN

0 1   5   10m

4

5

6

7

8

9

10

Senopati

Design/Completion: 1997/un-built
Jakarta, Republic of Indonesia
Grup Brasali
1,246,976 square feet/115,890 square meters
Precast concrete
Curtainwall, metal cladding

Senopati, a design for a multi-use complex in Jakarta, uses curved shapes to create a sophisticated interplay between its four-level, retail-mall base, and the clean and modern masses of office and residential towers. The mall curves inside two of the streets defining the site's footprint, to create a more dynamic space than would a more common "L" shape, while improving visual access in the mall's interior. Three atriums – one at the main entrance with a second-level food court, and two on the wings beneath distinctive sphere and cube skylights – aid

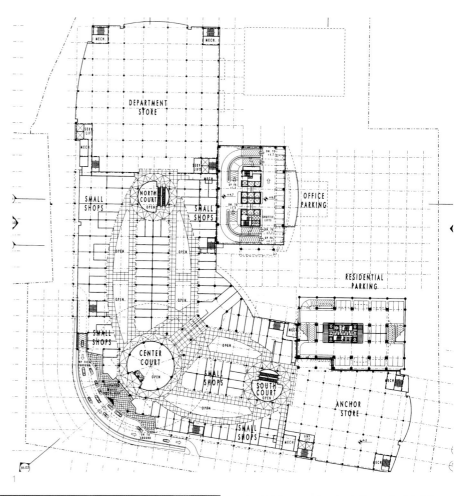

1

navigation and orientation. A third-floor, multi-screen cinema and a department store anchor the mall. High-tech advertising panels on its exterior are designed for slide and video ad displays.

The three-level mall is the podium for a 40-story office tower and a 28-story residential tower. The office tower is sleek and modern, solid in form with punched windows oriented toward the Indonesian sun. A sculpted, curved mass with expanses of glazed curtainwall helps to break up the solid rectangularity of the tower while creating a visual connection to the mall base. This design prevents the tower from appearing too massive, even though its rectangular footprint carries all the way to the top floor without tapering. The residential tower uses simple, clean shapes, integrating exterior stone panel walls and glass curtainwalls. Balconies carved into the wall add variety to the façade while offering residents views of the surrounding urban landscape.

2

Imagery:
1   Site plan
2   North elevation
3   Napkin sketch
4&5   Project massing

4

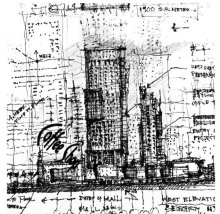

3

5

Kebon Melati

Design/Completion: 1996/un-built
Jakarta, Republic of Indonesia
PT Setdco Grahamandura/Trisranana
Sumbaga
28,000,000 square feet/2,602,230 square
meters
Reinforced concrete, steel
Curtainwalls of glass and aluminium, stone
cladding

There is an almost otherworldly feel to Kebon Melati, a master-plan design for a new city center in Jakarta. It is tempting to attribute this to the design's most prominent feature, a giant, glass atrium pyramid at its center, but it goes deeper than that. The reason may lie in the fact that the inspiration for this ultra-modern, mixed-use development comes from one of the most revered landmarks of ancient Indonesian culture: Borobudur, a 9th-century Buddhist–Hindu temple whose design was intended to symbolize the structure of the universe.

Kebon Melati integrates 10 floors of retail, entertainment, housing, recreation, and business uses on a 26-hectare (64-acre) site. Two office towers and a conference center anchor the northern end, with a waterside hotel at the north-east corner and apartments to the north-west. An atrium-covered walkway feeds into the central pyramid, which covers the shopping and entertainment complex. The pyramid takes its shape from traditional Indonesian house roof style. Two stepped apartment towers rise from the pyramid on the eastern side, with three more further south, all oriented toward the water and a waterside promenade. The south-west corner is a hotel complex, and two more office towers anchor the southern end. A triangular hotel complex sits inside the pyramid, its peak jutting through one of the pyramid panels. The project was planned to be built in three distinct phases.

Influenced by the Gupta architecture of India, Borobudur consisted of a series of stepped stone terraces leading to a large stupa, or Buddhist shrine, at its center. This influence is evident throughout Kebon Melati, seen in the façades of its towers, and in the stepped terraces leading to the pyramid, which, in effect, replaces the central shrine.

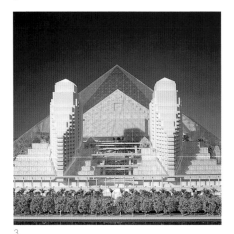

Imagery:	1	Promenade from above
	2	Shopping/ entertainment complex
	3	Atrium structure
	4	View toward conference center
	5	Canal promenade
	6	Site plan
Opposite		Site model

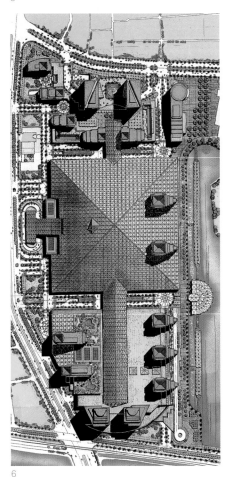

ALDHIYAFA

CAVENDISH SQUARE

CENTRO YBOR

EASTON TOWN CENTER

INTERNATIONAL COUNCIL OF SHOPPING CENTERS

MENLYN PARK

MILLENNIA

MUVICO THEATERS

NEWPORT ON THE LEVEE

POINTE ORLANDO

PRINT GRAPHICS AND LOGOS

TAIMALL

THE ZONE @ ROSEBANK

GRAPHICS

Aldhiyafa

Current project
Makkah, Saudi Arabia

Imagery:
1 Project logo
2 Medical building
3 Site perimeter banners
4 Concept elevation
5 Garage entry sign
6 Entrance gateway
7 Directory

Creating a graphic identity for the first major shopping mall in the Saudi Arabian holy city of Makkah posed some unique design challenges. The powerful regional influence of Makkah as a religious center prompted efforts to incorporate related symbols into the design, but in ways that would attract visitors to the mall without being offensive to those of Islamic faith. The logo resolves this problem by using an abstraction of religious shapes, with the outer square symbolizing the holy mosque's arena, the circle reflecting pilgrims' required circumambulations, and the inner square inspired by the sacred sanctuary of Kaaba at the mosque's center. The strong skewed shapes and colors – lime, bright orange, dark blue, and white – reflect the mall's contemporary tone.

The logo creates both a graphic identity and a powerful sense of place, sending a constant reminder to visitors that they are in Makkah. Because of this, the logo is used everywhere – abstracted in banners, directional signs, suspended forms, and other elements. Even directories use skewed forms derived from the logo.

2

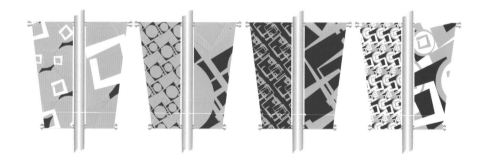

3

1

4

DEVELOPMENT **DESIGN GROUP** INCORPORATED

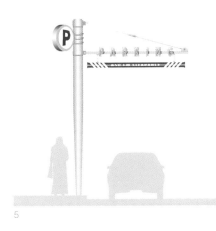

5

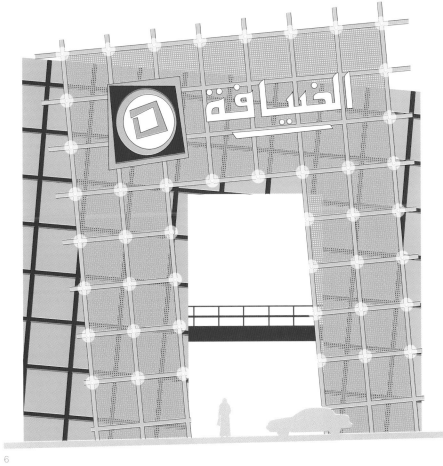

6

7

FEATURE GATE
(OPTION 4 SHOWN)

Cavendish Square

Design/Completion: 1997/1999
Cape Town, Republic of South Africa

Imagery:
1 Façade detail
2 Exterior banner concepts
3 Food court
4 Directory concept
5 Project logo
6 Exterior façade

Exterior feature graphics in a range of shapes, forms, and colors play a key role in Design Group's transformation of this formerly monolithic structure into an inviting, contemporary shopping mall. Banners and 3-D illuminated wall panels display the center's new sun-and-ray design theme in red, gold, orange, purple, and turquoise. Prominent steel canopies mark the entrances, and up-lighting displays the Cavendish Square name. Distinctive, curving torch lights brighten the façade. All combine to help this former imposing box become a bright and intriguing Cape Town retail destination.

Inside, forms and colors repeat the theme of the exterior. The designs reinforce the frequent contemporary abstractions of traditional African forms and patterns found in Cavendish Square's architectural features.

The Cavendish Square logo underscores the mall's dramatic makeover. The minimalist block "C", with its square negative space and the dropped out square below make a simple and effective statement about the center's new contemporary identity.

1

2

CAVENDISH SQUARE

3

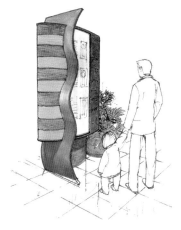

4

6

5

Centro Ybor

Design/Completion: 1996/2000
Tampa, Florida, USA

Imagery:
1 Wall mural
2 Directory ground graphic
3 Gateway façade
4 Directory
5 Project logo

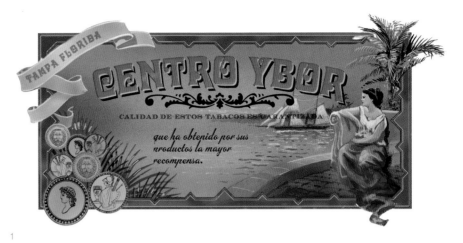

1

2

The graphic features of Centro Ybor, a festive night-time entertainment and retail district in Ybor City, near Tampa, Florida, reflect the city's past as the first cigar-making factory town in the US. Research on the cigar culture of the late 19th and early 20th centuries led to the logo design, the bronze, blue-green, and red color palette, and the choice of the typeface. Bold red "Centro Ybor" signs, highlighted with neon and Tivoli lights, accent the exterior, and complement Centro Ybor's Spanish Colonial architecture.

The use of bronze in signage, and wrought iron in gates, railings, and sign panels reflect Centro Ybor's geographic and historical setting. A secondary "CY" logo displayed at the center of a medallion is a frequent design element, appearing in iron gates and railings, and as a bronze-inlaid floor design. An inlaid bronze-and-mosaic-tile floor graphic with a striking sun design at its center marks a central directory. Wall murals pick up on the cigar label theme.

3

4

5

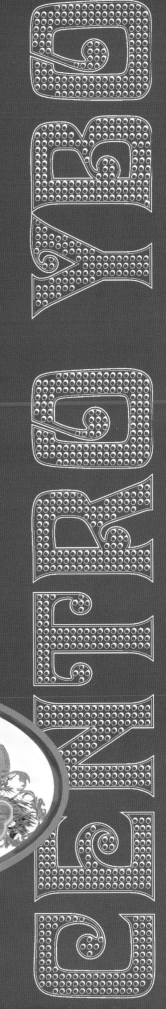

Easton Town Center

Design/Completion: 1996/1999
Columbus, Ohio, USA

Imagery:
1 Street scene
2 Billboard mural
3 Directory
4 Garage entry sign
5 Town Square
6 Vehicular directional

1

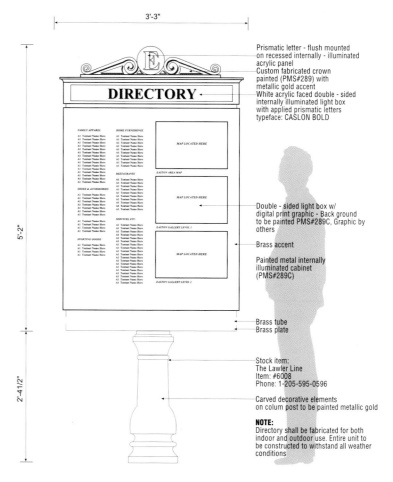

3'-3"

DIRECTORY

Prismatic letter - flush mounted on recessed internally - illuminated acrylic panel

Custom fabricated crown painted (PMS#289) with metallic gold accent

White acrylic faced double - sided internally illuminated light box with applied prismatic letters typeface: CASLON BOLD

Double - sided light box w/ digital print graphic - Back ground to be painted PMS#289C, Graphic by others

Brass accent

Painted metal internally illuminated cabinet (PMS#289C)

Brass tube
Brass plate

Stock item:
The Lawler Line
Item: #6008
Phone: 1-205-595-0596

Carved decorative elements on colum post to be painted metallic gold

NOTE:
Directory shall be fabricated for both indoor and outdoor use. Entire unit to be constructed to withstand all weather conditions

3

2

6

Conservative graphics reinforce the "All-American" theme of this neo-traditional town center. Simple, elegant, and easy-to-read wayfinding signage components direct and orient visitors around the streets and public spaces. A carved limestone "Est. 1999" building plaque tells visitors of this small town's short historic past. A patriotic color palette of red, white, and blue can be found throughout.

While most graphic components have been designed to blend with their surroundings, some bolder elements reflect America's love of nostalgia. The parking garage identification sign mounted above the entry portal, for instance, takes its shape and design from signs found along American highways of the 1950s.

4

5

International Council of Shopping Centers

Various dates
Las Vegas, USA

Imagery:
1. Head table conceptual model
2. 1999 head table detail
3. 1999 head table

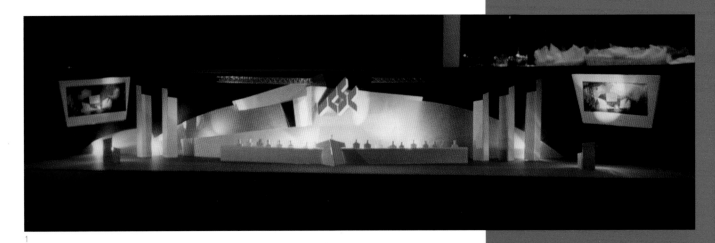

1

Design Group creates the graphics, convention floor layout, and promotional materials for the International Council of Shopping Centers' annual Spring Convention, which draws some 35,000 convention-goers to Las Vegas each spring. Most years this means creating a graphic design theme for the event and applying it to collateral materials, promotional kits, feature graphics, and wayfinding elements in the convention hall. Every fifth year, however, the firm completely reconstructs the convention hall stage set to create an entirely new interior space.

Design Group's convention experience includes booth design and layout for several exhibitors at the ICSC Spring Convention.

2

4

5

6

7

Imagery:
4 Information kiosk
5 Association booth
6 Exterior banner
7 Food court
8 Exhibitor booth
9 "Shopperama"
10 "Shopperama" concept elevation

8

9

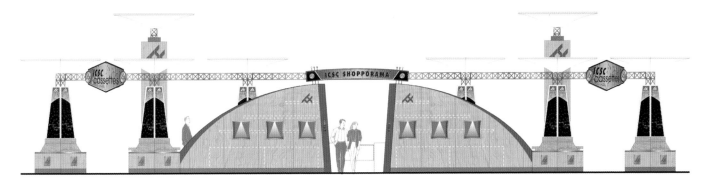

10

Menlyn Park

Design/Completion: 1997/2000
Pretoria, Republic of South Africa

Imagery:
1 Directory
2 Food court identity
3 Entry signage
4 Garage identity
5 Interior sculpture
6 Menlyn events
7 Project pylon

Perhaps the most distinctive architectural feature of the Menlyn Park shopping and entertainment center is the tensile fabric roof that covers its Grand Hall. The tent-like roof inspired the Menlyn Park logo, whose overlapping tent wings also form an abstract "M" for "Menlyn." The wing shape recurs throughout the center, found in stretched fabric panels, distinctive lighting fixtures, and banners.

Menlyn Park's architecture creates heavily themed identities for each of its various halls, and the graphic elements reinforce these themes. Feature planet-and-star graphics, and fiber-optic accented constellations in a turquoise sky mark the Celestial Hall. The planet-and-star motif is also found in the hall's etched-glass railing panels, and in a spherical sundial sculpture. Suspended, fabric wing shapes take flight in the Aviary Hall. In Restaurant Row, a 3-D place setting goes awry, as though the tablecloth had been pulled out from under.

Because of Menlyn Park's size (it has more than 100,000 square meters of retail space), wayfinding is an important concern. Bold and colorful directional and identification signs guide visitors around the project site, a six-level parking garage, and the mall's interior.

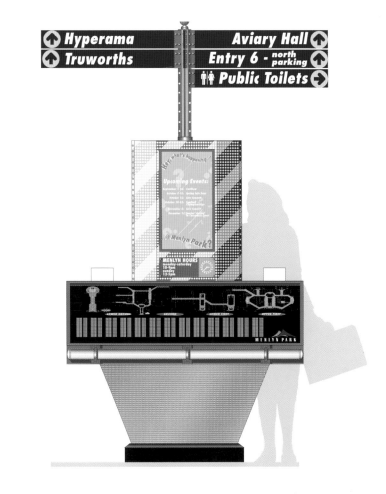

1

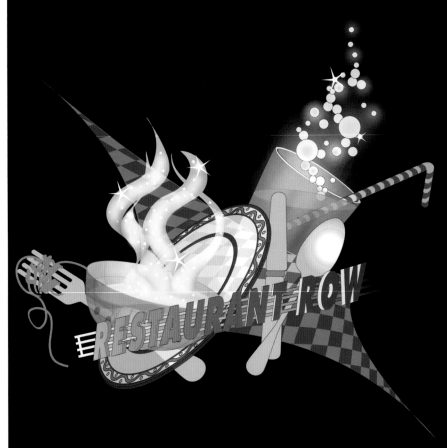

2

3

4

5

6

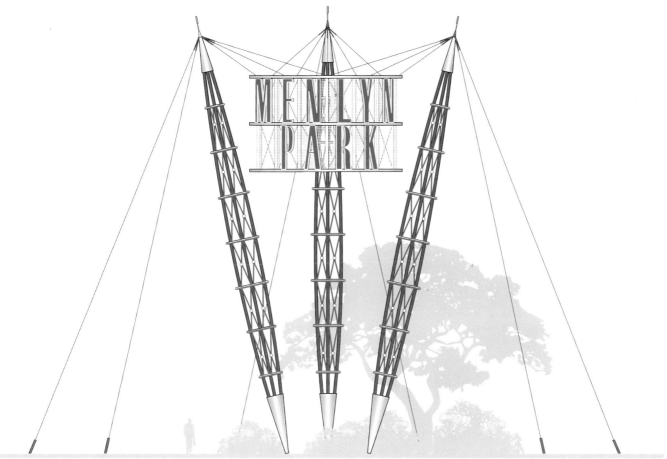

7

Millennia

Design/Completion: 1998/2000
Ankara, Turkey

Imagery:
1	Directory
2	Project logo
2	Feature sculpture
4	Exterior banners
5	Concept elevation

The graphic design plan for this retail and hotel complex under construction in Ankara, Turkey, reflects its futuristic name and contemporary architecture. The word "millennia" is about time, and implies movement toward the future. The logo, an abstract clock in cobalt blue and gold, captures this futuristic theme simply and effectively. The logo works well paired with the project typeface, or independently as a recognizable icon.

The clock motif, found in banners, signs, etched-glass accents, wall panels, and a granite-and-marble inlaid floor design, is one prominent feature. Another is Millennia Man, displayed in a two-dimensional exterior metal sculpture, where he holds an etched-glass Millennia medallion, lit with fiber optics. Millennia Man introduces a distinctive curved shape into the Millennia graphics plan. Banner designs, curved directory display stands, garage wall graphics, and signage are among the many places that use this curve effectively.

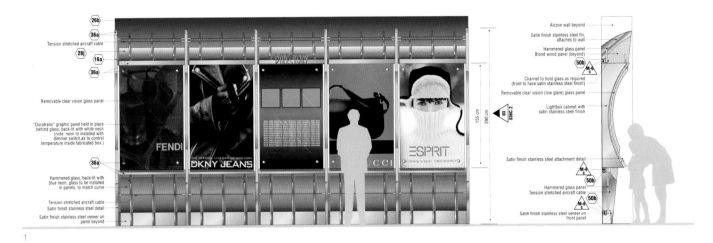

1

2

3

5

4

Muvico Theaters

Various dates
Various locations in the USA

Imagery:

1 Muvico Paradise 24
   entry pylon
2 Muvico Paradise 24
   porte-cochere
3 Muvico Paradise 24
   wall mural
4 Muvico Tampa
   Palms arcade
   identity
5 Muvico Pompano
   concessions
6 Muvico Centro Ybor
   decorative banners
7 Muvico Pompano
   concessions

1

The graphic designs for the multiplex cinema complexes being developed around the country by Muvico Theaters generally take one of two directions. In some cases the graphics have a subordinate role, existing to inform and direct moviegoers, and generally to complement a strong architectural statement. The graphics for Muvico Paradise 24 enhance the theater's powerful Egyptian-theme architecture, but don't compete with it. Graphic subtlety is also the approach at other, differently themed Muvico theaters, including those at the company's Ybor City, Baywalk, and Boca Raton locations.

At other times, however, the architecture becomes a backdrop for the feature graphics that define a place and theme. "Motel" signs, diner food icons, neon, Tivoli lighting, and other elements help create the 1950s drive-in theme for Muvico Pompano. Train graphics, a railroad-crossing marquee, and track-number cinema signs do the same for the railroad-themed Muvico Peabody Place 22. At these complexes, graphics alone create the fantasy world signature that has become Muvico Theaters' trademark.

2

3

4

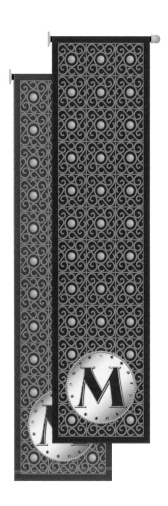

6

5

7

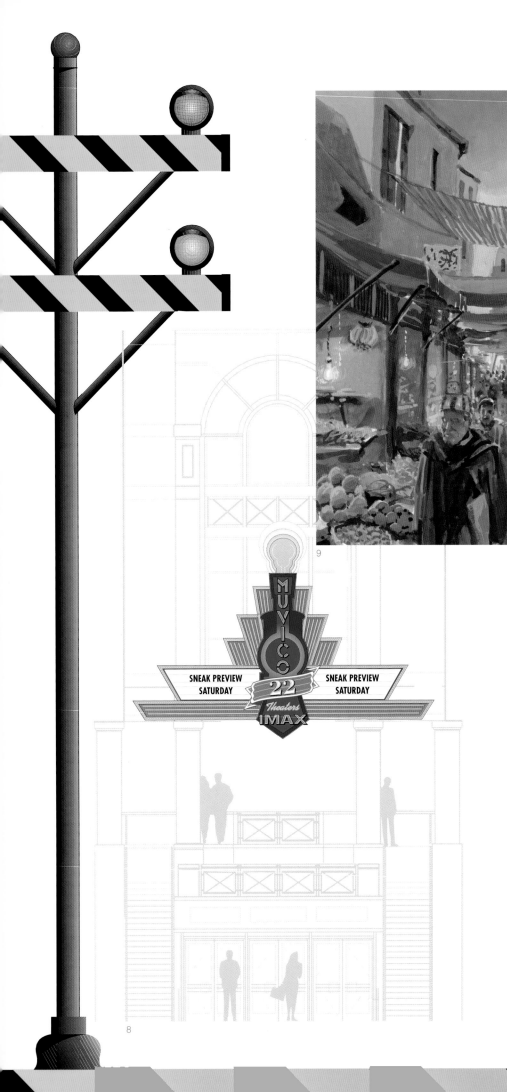

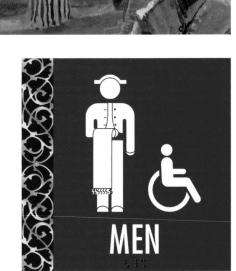

MEN

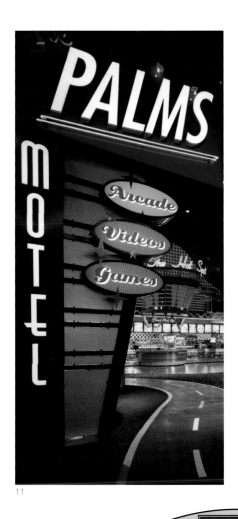

11

12

Newport on the Levee

Design/Completion: 1997/2001
Newport, Kentucky, USA

Imagery:
1 Directory
2 Exterior identification sign
3 Kinetic sculpture
4 Entertainment zone graphics
5 Promenade medallion
6 Upper plaza
7 Sculpture topiary

3

The graphic theme for this riverfront retail and entertainment center pays homage to the American industrial-era factories and workers that once were located here on the banks of the Ohio River. Metal and industrial icons have been oxidized to create the sense that they may have been produced in factories from the earlier era. The project makes generous use of natural materials such as bronze and copper, and celebrates such industrial elements as rivets, bolts, and other structural attachments. A prominent feature is an illuminated, 11-foot-high "Newport" sign, promoting the city of Newport and the project's identity across the river to neighboring Cincinnati, Ohio, on the opposite shore.

1

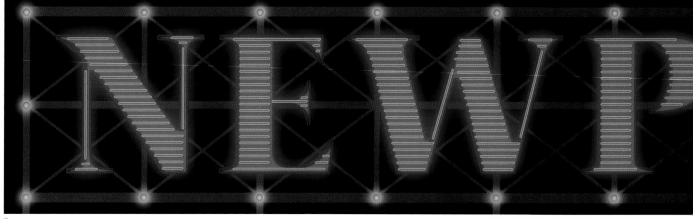

2

4

5

6

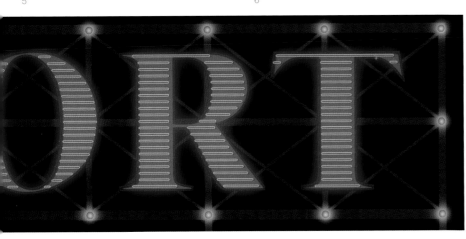

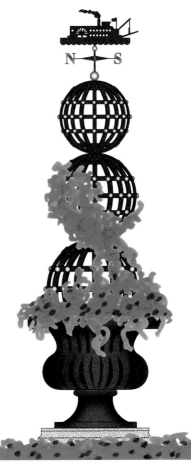

7

Pointe Orlando

Design/Completion: 1998/unbuilt
Orlando, Florida, USA

Imagery:
1. Promenade graphics
2. Exterior pole-mounted banner
3. Exterior identification sign
4. Fantasy icons
5. Promenade sculptures

The graphic design plan for Pointe Orlando, a commercial center in Orlando's convention district, aims to create an identity for the center itself that both supports and is distinct from the identity projected by its major tenants. Fuschia, lime, pink, and other colors running from warm to hot add new energy, and enliven the existing center logo. Sculptures of abstracted marine forms – waves, fish, mermaids, shells – accent a central promenade at key points along a serpentine fountain, and create an aquatic theme for Pointe Orlando. The forms are repeated throughout the center, in welcome signs, in banners, in an inlaid floor design, and in fabric "waves" suspended from the ceiling above the promenade.

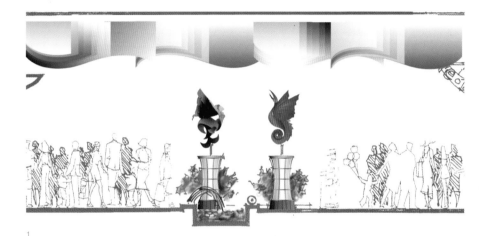

1

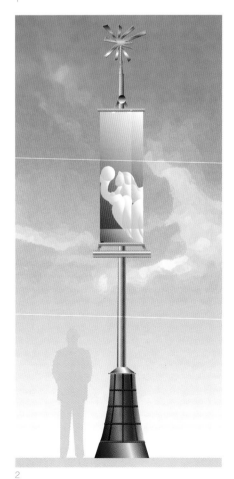

2

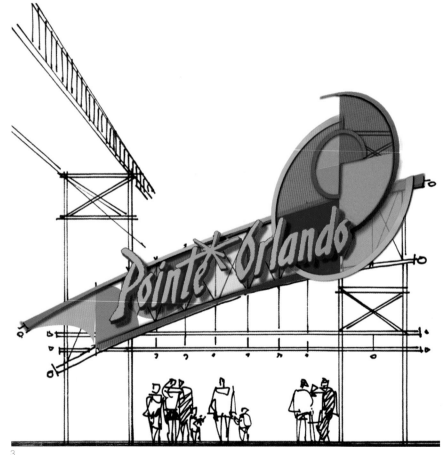

3

Imagery:

1 1999 DDG holiday calender

2 Identity stationary package

3 ICSC Millennium World Congress brochures/mailers 2000

Opposite Various logo designs

1

2

3

Design Group's print graphics portfolio includes collateral and mass-mailing brochures, leasing booklets for commercial projects, and the firm's own promotional materials. Purpose, use, and audience are the core factors that influence design. Attention to color, composition, and contrast create layouts that are direct, clear, and balanced, and that contain elements of surprise to hold a reader's interest.

Design Group aims to create logos that are memorable and timeless. Their inspiration may come from a variety of sources, such as a project's name, its geographical setting, or the history and culture of the region in which it's located. Whatever the motivating influence, the objective is to create an aesthetically satisfying and easily recognizable icon that quickly and simply captures the identity of a place.

AL DHIYAFA

PALMERA
CAIRO EGYPT

STREETS ·OF· MAYFAIR

Join Us
IN GOOD COMPANY

Mariner's Cove
GÖCEK TURKEY

MENLYN PARK

FAIRFAX
CORNER

Beachside
ARUBA

EXPO
XPLORE

MENARA
KEMAYORAN

CHELSEA
MARKET
ESTABLISHED
1998

THE ZONE
ROSEBANK

Tai Mall

Design/Completion: 1998/1999
Taipei, Taiwan

Imagery:
1 Façade detail
2 Typical mall banners
3 Directional
4 Interior banners
5 Exterior façade
6 Project logo

1

3

2

4

6

Research into the medieval era led to the development of graphics for Tai Mall that complement the building's castle theme. The logo uses the Chinese character for the word "Tai"; its presentation as a Chinese signature reflects Tai Mall's cultural setting, while also evoking a medieval crest or shield.

Medieval tapestries inspired the design of pole-mounted triangular banners around the building's exterior. Their blues, golds, purples, and deep burgundy reds are colors authentic to the medieval era, while their graphic elements add contemporary accents. Finding that balance between medieval and contemporary was one of the main challenges designers faced in creating the graphics.

Throughout, Tai Mall's graphics are elegant, functional, and subtle, providing a quieter backdrop to the building's bold architectural features. This approach augments the overall theme, without competing with those features.

5

The Zone@Rosebank

Design/Completion: 1998/2000
Johannesburg, Republic of South Africa

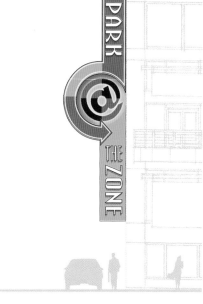

2

Imagery:
1   Banner/poster case
2   Garage entry sign
3   Exterior façade
4   Project logo
5   Concept elevation

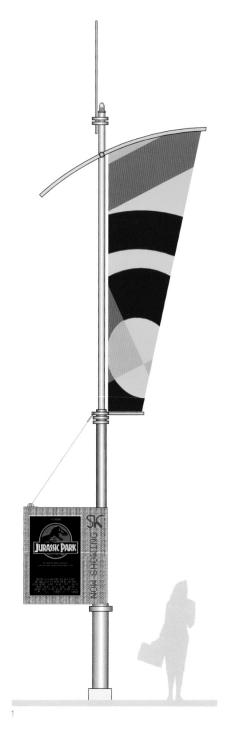

1

In some cases, graphic design takes a secondary role, serving simply as a subtle complement to a building's architectural features. With the Zone@Rosebank, it is the architecture that takes something of a back seat to the bold graphic expressions promoting the complex and its tenants.

The logo's use of the "@" symbol reflects Rosebank's high energy and high-tech atmosphere, while its simple forms and bold, flat areas of color show the influence of South African patterns and designs. The symbol is powerful enough visually to stand on its own in many locations, without the "Rosebank" name. The symbol is so recognizable, that even the partial display of its shapes and colors in banners, directional signs, and entrance elements communicates the Rosebank identity.

A three-sided Zone@Rosebank tower at a pivotal intersection, and prominent feature graphics along the façades stand out in the graphically intense exterior. Parking@Rosebank signs use the logo and wordplay to denote car entry points. Large, illuminated fabric advertising panels on the Oxford Road façade promote tenants and bring in advertising revenue. Strict tenant design criteria prevent the admittedly loud streetscape from becoming a confusing cacophony of typeface, shape, and color.

3

4

DUBAI BLUE COAST

DREAMLAND MASTER PLAN

PRIVATE RESIDENTIAL LANDSCAPE

JOHANNESBURG MASTER PLAN

USARTS DISTRICT

KEMER COUNTRY

KOTA LEGENDA

MARINER'S COVE

PANTAI KAPUKNAGA

TABA GOLDEN COAST

TARUMA RESORT

TELAGA KAHURIPAN

ZONK'IZIZWE

PLANNING

Dubai Blue Coast

Design/Completion: 1996
Dubai, United Arab Emirates
Al Ghurair Group
46 acres/18.6 ha

Imagery:
1   Master Plan
2   Promenade
3   The Bazaar
4   Hillside Villas
5   Swimming Lagoon
6   Jogging trails
7   Marina

Viewed from above, the most distinctive feature of the master plan for the Dubai Blue Coast resort on the Arabian Gulf is a curved breakwater that arcs into the Gulf. The breakwater doubles as a promenade leading to a lighthouse and restaurant at its end. This strong and elegant shape defines the resort's intimate relationship with the sea.

Behind the breakwater is an island with a marina and a marketplace inspired by Arabian vernacular architecture. Seawall bridges separate the marina from

a swimming area and connect it to the mainland, leading to a courtyard at one end and a sports center at the other.

Houses and villas are scattered over a created hillside sloping to the sea. The natural coastal terrain is extremely flat, so the design calls for building the hillside, which has the dual benefit of adding views of the Gulf from the residences while creating space beneath the residences for below-grade parking. The overall design encourages pedestrian movement inside the resort; there are only two modest roads, one

1

winding to the promenade and the other to the sports center and a health spa. Of particular note is a bird sanctuary created within the new landscape design. Residences range from large, luxury villas to more modest eco-cottages built in a vernacular stone-and-stucco style, with corner towers to facilitate natural air circulation.

2

3

4

5

6

7

Dreamland Master Plan

Design/Completion: 1998/under
construction
Cairo, Egypt
The Bahgat Group
Golf architect: Karl Litten, Inc.
2,100 acres/850 hectares

The Master Plan for Dreamland calls for the creation of a comprehensive community integrating a range of residential, business, recreational, and entertainment uses. Throughout the 850-hectare (2,100-acre) site are a retail and entertainment center (described in the Entertainment section, page 56), high- and medium-density residences at a variety of price ranges, office space, a high-tech research park, and resorts oriented around golf, health and fitness, and the equestrian arts. Less than an hour's drive from Cairo, Dreamland integrates these various uses with the surrounding landscape, to create an organized community for more than 100,000 residents, and a resort destination for citizens of Cairo and the region.

The equestrian resort has a polo club and field, dressage arena, steeplechase course, and stables for up to 200 horses. The Health Resort integrates 1,500 residential units with a spa, hospital, high-tech office park, and a nine-hole golf course. The richly landscaped golf resort provides apartment and villa

residents with easy access to a championship golf course and a commercial center, and also includes a golf hotel, and convention and conference facilities.

Abundant water features throughout Dreamland are welcome in the arid desert climate. The plan uses the natural topography to create enhance views of one of the most stunning features in the world's built landscape: the Pyramids of Giza, eight kilometers to the east. In fact, the community's central organizing axis was positioned specifically to create pyramid vistas for those in Dreamland's residential and commercial areas.

Construction on several phases began in 1999.

Imagery: 1   Golf view
            Below   Master plan

1

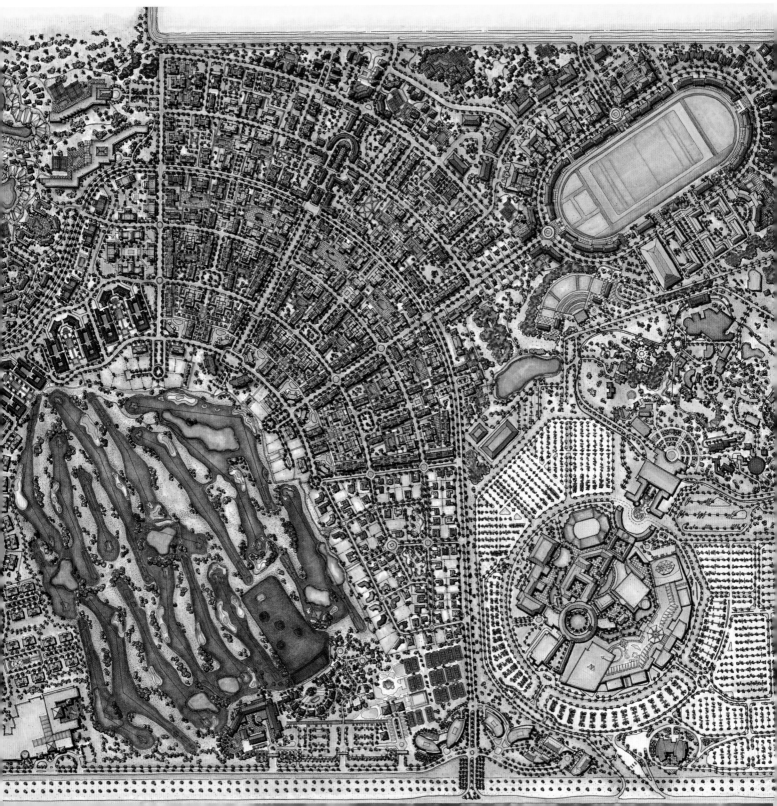

3

4

5

6

7

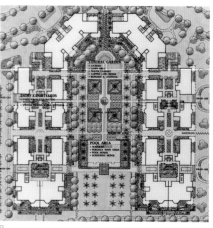

8

9

10

Private Residential Landscape

Design/Completion 1990/1992
Olde Severna Park, Maryland
Client undisclosed

The use of terraces and a range of indigenous flora transform this Annapolis hillside into a lush garden landscape. The terraces resolved a problem posed by the site's topography, with its nine-meter (30-foot) change in grade. An upper terrace, with a fieldstone patio and goldfish pond, connects to the main living area of the house. It overlooks a lower pool terrace.

Plantings offer a wide spectrum of colors and textures. Borrowing an approach found in many Asian gardens, the landscape uses leaf color to maintain a full palette, even during seasons when flowers are not in bloom. Closely planted Northern Bayberry and natural grasses common to Maryland's Eastern Shore add privacy. Flowers and shrubs include daylilies, hyacinth, tickseed, photinia, black-eyed Susan, English laurel, mountain laurel, rhododendron, and azalea. Flowering trees such as cherry, redbud, dogwood, and maple add a burst of spring color. Persimmon, oak, and black walnut round out the landscape. The rich diversity has created a popular habitat for local wildlife, attracting raccoon, deer, opossum, and a wide variety of birds, including the occasional eagle.

1

2

3

Imagery:
1 Front entry
2 Garden dining
   terrace
3 Garden steps
4 Pool terrace
5 View toward pool
   terrace

4

5

Johannesburg Revitalization

Design/Completion: 1996/on-going
Johannesburg, Republic of South Africa
Central Johannesburg Partnership
1,433 acres/580 hectares

Imagery:
1   Design charrette
2   Master plan

1

In the mid-1990s, during a time of sweeping cultural change in South Africa, the Central Johannesburg Partnership sought Design Group's help in coordinating a planning process that would play an important role in revitalizing a city that had experienced a period of decline. A team of designers, planners, and architects met with major stakeholders, and undertook a comprehensive survey of the city, using figure-ground analysis, traffic studies, and other methods to examine such urban phenomena as land-use patterns, population density, and traffic circulation, among others. The process revealed underused areas and vacant properties throughout the downtown grid, places that people avoid, and places that inhibit access to other parts of the city.

The resulting plan makes recommendations for new or upgraded uses in five key regions, creating business improvement districts throughout downtown Johannesburg. New tenants would be sought for retail stores in blocks surrounding a north-city transportation hub. The transportation center itself would be re-planned, and a new retail and entertainment district would replace a former bus station parking lot. A new streetscape and other enhancements would revitalize a merchandise mart to the south, and a wholesale trading district to the east. A western district would become an arts community, with gallery and loft space, and new restaurants. These changes on the perimeter would energize a central district of government offices and retail stores, which itself would undergo a facelift. Though designed to produce significant change in the city, the recommendations minimized disruption by reflecting established usage patterns.

Changes of this nature, with many stakeholders, often move slowly, but Johannesburg is applying concepts in the plan, and is beginning to experience a renaissance.

2

1

2

Design/Completion: 1996/on-going
Washington, DC, USA
Mayor's Office, City of Washington, DC
375 acres/152 hectares

Imagery:
1 7th Street from MCI Center
2 Streetscape
3 Vision plan

The American capital city of Washington, DC is one of the nation's most popular tourist destinations, attracting millions of visitors each year from around the globe. A commercial district north of a central tourist spine, however, had benefited little from the influx of visitors, prompting the formation in the mid-1990s of a task force to find ways to revitalize it.

As a member of that task force, Design Group synthesized the work of several committees into a plan for the USArts District, a blueprint for a vibrant, mixed-use region of commerce, entertainment, and the arts. An existing art gallery, a planned professional sports arena (since completed) and convention center, and other city strengths serve as springboards for a comprehensive re-merchandising of the district. A major train/bus/subway inter-modal transportation hub, adjacent to the World Town free trade zone, would improve access to the district. A former convention center would become the American Entertainment Center, anchoring an arts-and-entertainment sector in the district's center. Several new interactive museums, including a children's museum, would be added.

These changes would bring increased retail spending, added safety, and economic security in surrounding neighborhoods, and new job opportunities. In all, the plan deploys strategic and complementary uses in order to breathe new life into a region feeling the effects of urban under-use.

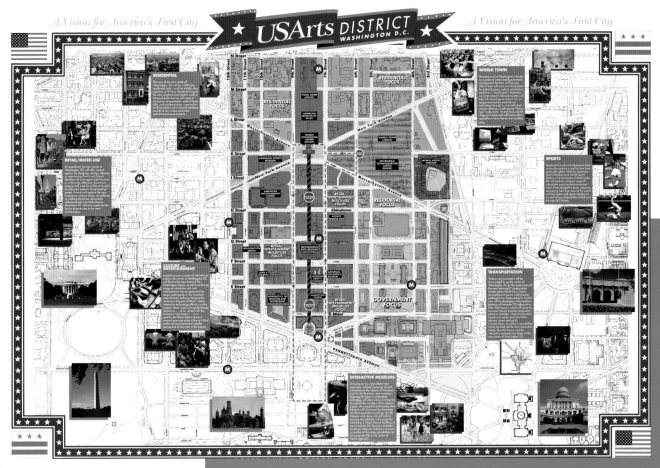

3

Kemer Country

Design/Completion: 1995/1997
Istanbul, Turkey
Kemer Yapit Ve Turizm A.S.
182 acres/17 hectares
Concrete frame
Masonry, stucco, timber, and clay tile
roofing

The design for Kemer Country, a luxury golf and equestrian community near Istanbul, involves the creative integration of existing natural and human-made forms with a new built environment. Using a site surrounded by mountains and a national forest preserve, the design adapts an ancient Roman aqueduct, originally used to bring water to Istanbul, into a prominent perimeter landmark. The central valley has become a golf course community, with different types of medium- and high-density housing oriented around the golf course at various elevations.

A prominent feature is a central, artificial lake, which would be filled with water found beneath that part of the site.

Kemer's housing is a contemporary translation of traditional Turkish styles. There are four types of housing: townhouses, tightly grouped villas, three-level condominiums, and apartments in a six-story building near the lake. The layout maximizes views of, and proximity to, the lake, creating a Turkish hillside village with stone privacy walls lining its streets. A central courtyard with a pool serves as a community gathering place.

Below-ground parking garages serve the high-density residential areas.

Housing prototypes call for concrete, stone, and brick construction, stucco siding, and tile roofs. Elements such as terra cotta fountains, and the extensive use of natural wood reflect traditional regional influences. The orientation and sensitive siting of structures, and the design's attention to details help connect Kemer Country to the surrounding topography and to Turkish culture.

3

Imagery:
1 Site plan
2 View toward aqueduct
3 Main street
4 Lakeside condominiums
5 Villa apartment pool
6 Villa apartments lakeside elevation

4

5

6

Kota Legenda

Design/Completion: 1995/under
construction
Bekasi, Republic of Indonesia
PT Putra Alvita Pratama
Golf architects: Arnold Palmer, PCDC and
JMP Golf Design Group
6,669 acres/2,700 hectares

1

Planners turned Indonesian land-use regulations that prohibit development on pre-existing agricultural areas into a design asset for Kota Legenda, a new town outside of Jakarta. The ecologically sensitive design avoids disrupting former rice paddies in the center of the 2,700-hectare (6,700-acre) site, and uses the water that feeds them to create lakes and other waterways in and around two 18-hole golf courses.

Surrounding the golf courses are themed residential villages, each with its own schools, day care centers, neighborhood centers, and variety of housing types. Conceived to help alleviate overcrowding in Jakarta, Kota Legenda is designed to accommodate 210,000 residents in homes built in Balinese, Western Colonial, Mediterranean, Greek, and other vernacular styles. Housing is a blend of low-, medium-, and high-density residential units. Other community features include a hospital, a business park (with a nine-hole executive golf course), a major commercial center, and an international school.

The name Kota Legenda comes in part from the legends-of-the-world monuments that mark the village plazas. Structures reminiscent of the Eiffel Tower, the Taj Mahal, the Pyramids of Giza, the Statue of Liberty, and Borobudur, a Hindu–Buddhist temple on the island of Java, create neighborhood identities, and help orient residents throughout the community.

Pacific Coast Builders Conference Gold Nugget Award, Grand Award – Best Land Plan, 1995

2

3

4

5

Imagery:

1 Typical high-density residence
2 Golf/marina clubhouse
3 Residential neighborhood
4 Lakeside restaurant illustration
5 Canal front neighborhood
6 Town center
7 Village schematic diagram
8 Master plan

6

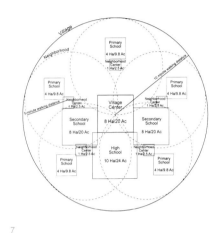

7

8

Mariner's Cove

Design/Completion: 1998/on-going
Göcek, Turkey
Enternasyonal Tourism Investments, Inc.
54 acres/22 hectares

1

Mariner's Cove, on Fethiye Bay along the Aegean Coast, challenged designers to take maximum advantage of a stunning hillside setting while remaining sensitive to the environment and adhering to strict local building codes. The resort, designed for one of the world's most beautiful yachting destinations, integrates a commercial center near the village of Göcek, a 400-berth marina, a yacht club, 125 villas, and a luxury hotel.

A more typical approach for this steep site would have been to construct a single hotel building, but zoning codes placed severe restrictions on building dimensions and the amount of land any single structure could cover. The solution was to build the hotel as a many-layered, Old World hill town, with multi-unit dwellings and villas spread over a hillside thick with pines. Transportation within the hotel complex is by foot or by golf-cart-like vehicles that are gentle on the landscape. A funicular takes guests to a restaurant at the site's highest point, near the hotel villas. The hotel layout uses hillside topography to maximize views of the bay.

The commercial center is in a Mediterranean style, with stucco-sided, tile-roofed buildings oriented around central plazas. One striking design feature is a canal that brings water in from the bay to a half-moon fountain pool in the center plaza, creating a welcoming community gathering space.

2

3

4

5

Imagery:
1   Commercial
2   Master plan
3   Yacht club
4   Mariner's walk
5   Resort villas
6   Hillside resort hotel
7   Village streetscape
8   Health spa
9   Hotel cottages
      section/elevation

6

7

8

Cottages

Path

Pine Forest

9

Pantai Kapuknaga

Design/Completion: 1992/under construction
West Java, Republic of Indonesia
Salim Group/PT Kapuknaga Indah
Consultants: NEDECO Engineering, The Netherlands; Traffic Group, Maryland, USA
25,000 acres/10,160 hectares

Imagery:
1 Master plan
2 Newport Place under construction

The master plan for this ambitious development will create a waterfront community on the Java Sea for more than 600,000 inhabitants. This sweeping development, which grew from an initial design for a more modest tourist community, will create a full-scale city composed of districts with their own distinct identities.

Watertown, with its distinctive central island, is Pantai Kapuknaga's commercial hub. The island is a duty-free shopping and recreation center attached by two bridges to the mainland. A marina provides services for visiting boaters. Grand Boulevard connects Watertown to Grand Canal, a mixed-use community with golf and other recreational amenities, a commercial sector, and a technology park. Research into some of the world's most notable waterfront cities helped to inspire the design for Grand Canal. The Boulevard itself is a lively venue for street performers, merchants, and other activity. Mariner's Cove, to the west, preserves and updates an existing fishing community, adding packaging and canning facilities to enhance the local industry. Next to Mariner's Cove is Turtle Coast, with its Turtle Walk

1

seafront promenade. East of Turtle Coast, Pacific Point Preserve wraps an eco-tourism resort around an existing mangrove forest.

Construction has begun on Newport Place, Pantai Kapuknaga's gateway to nearby Jakarta, to the east.

Pacific Coast Builders Conference Gold Nugget Award – Site Plan of the Year & Best of Show, 1992

Pacific Coast Builders Conference Gold Nugget Award, Grand Award – Best New Town Plan, 1992

2

JAVA SEA

WATERTOWN

- Harborfront Commercial District
- Leisure/Entertainment
- Duty Free Shopping
- Treasure Island
- Marina Kapuknaga
- International Marina
- Convention/Conference Centers
- 18 Hole Golf Course
- Luxury Waterfront Hotels
- Waterfront Resort Condominiums
- Yacht/Marina Country Clubs
- Recreational/Swimming Beaches
- Ocean View Mono Rail
- Inter-Island Ferry/Cruise Ship Shuttle Terminal

Cruise Ship Shuttle/Ferry Terminal

cial District

Waterfront Garden Apartments

Waterfront Estates

Sea Defense Dike

g Arts/Cultural Center

ermodal Transportation Hub

dical Research and Development Center

Regional Hospital

Medical Engineering & Science Institute

Corporate Office Campus

Gated Communities

High Technology Research and Development Park

GRAND CANAL

- Riverwalk Commercial District
- Corporate Headquarters
- Commercial Mixed Use
- Recreational Themed Resort
- 18 Hole Golf Course
- International Schools
- Private Swimming Lagoons
- Riverwalk Residential
- Residential Villas
- Garden Apartments/Condominiums
- Ocean View Mono Rail
- Light Rail Transit Center

Riverwalk Commercial District

Club Med

Waterfront Garden Apartments/Condominiums

NEWPORT PLACE

- Embassy Square
- International Trade Center
- Convention/Conference Centers
- Commercial & Mixed Use
- Business Offices
- Business Conference Hotels
- Village Centers
- Neighborhood Centers
- Gated Residential Villages

RIVER EAST

- Community Parks
- Health Clubs
- Commercial & Mixed Use
- International Schools
- Mediterranean Villages
- Village Centers
- Neighborhood Centers
- Courtyard Housing
- Waterfront Townhouses
- Waterfront Apartments/Condominiums

Rice Preserve

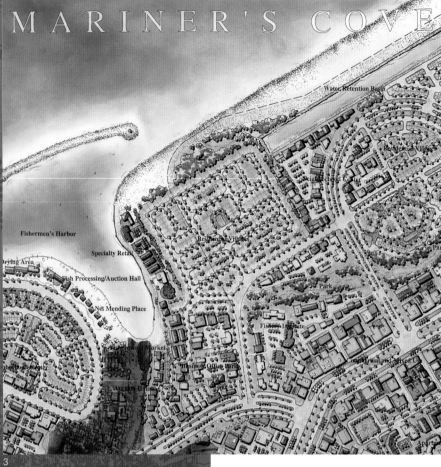

MARINER'S COVE

Water Retention Basin
Residential Villages
Neighborhood Center
Fishermen's Harbor
Specialty Retail
Drying Area
Fish Processing/Auction Hall
Net Mending Place
Residential Villages
Park
Park
Fishers Institute
Fishermen's Market
Neighborhood Center
Business Office Park
Commercial and Mixed Use
Auction House
Apartment

3

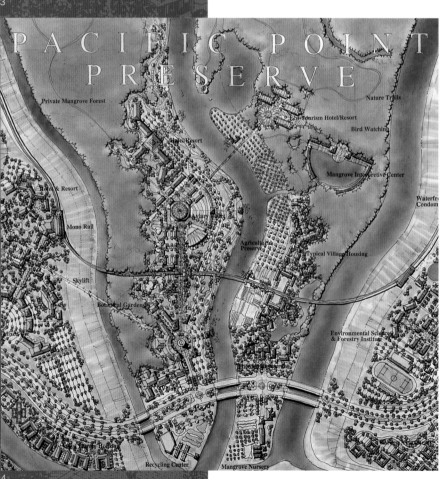

PACIFIC POINT PRESERVE

Private Mangrove Forest
Nature Trails
Eco-Tourism Hotel/Resort
Hotel/Resort
Bird Watching
Mangrove Interpretive Center
Beach & Resort
Waterfront Condos
Mono Rail
Agricultural Preserve
Typical Village Housing
Skylift
Botanical Gardens
Environmental Science & Forestry Institute
Village Center
Recycling Center
Mangrove Nursery

4

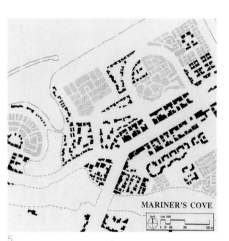

MARINER'S COVE

5

PACIFIC POINT PRESERVE

6

7

8

9

10

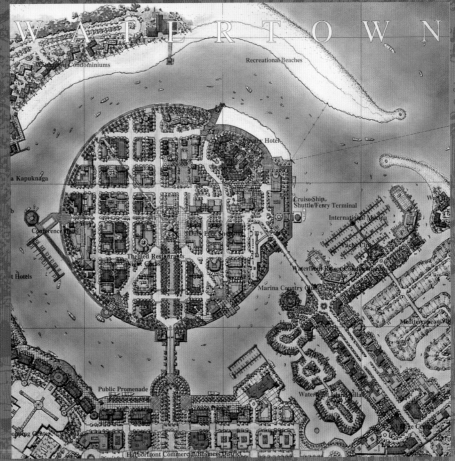

WATERTOWN

Condominiums
Recreational Beaches
Hotel
Cruise Ship
Shuttle/Ferry Terminal
International Marina
Conference Hall
Waterfront Resort Condominiums
Themed Restaurants
Marina Country Club
Mediterranean Villas
Public Promenade
Waterfront Island Villas
Harborfront Commercial/Business District

11

GRAND CANAL

Specialty Housing
Residential Villages
Front Villas
Resort Hotel/Cottages
Mono Rail
Residential Villages
Golf Club House
Commercial/Business District
Riverwalk
18 Hole Golf Course
International Schools
Swimming Lagoon
Neighborhood Center
Waterfront Island
Mixed Use Development
Golf Hotel/Resort

12

Taba Golden Coast

Design/Completion: 1997/under
construction
Taba, Egypt
SOFTD, Sixth of October for Tourism
Development
109 acres/44 hectares

Located on the Sinai Peninsula near Eilat, in an area where the typical resort complex might include a couple of hotels and some time-share residences, Taba Golden Coast creates a waterfront tourist village, combining hotels and vacation residences with marketplaces, day and night-time entertainment, and a wide array of other activities for visitors attracted to the white sandy beaches, and clear blue water of the Gulf of Aqaba.

A central waterway is both the Egyptian-themed resort's most distinctive landmark and a key organizing principle, extending from the welcome center at the resort entrance to the beachfront. The waterway becomes a stylized imitation of the Nile River, flowing past Aswan Center (retail stores and a market), Luxor Square (a spa, recreation, and night life), and Thebes Village (a town center with shops, cafés, and a park), before ending at the beachfront Cairo Delta markets and public plaza. From there, a diving platform juts into the water, accenting Taba's relationship with the gulf, and providing easy access to offshore coral formations for swimmers and divers.

Car traffic is limited to a perimeter road, and all resort components are linked by pedestrian pathways. The main highway and a beachfront promenade make it easy for vacationers at resorts to the north and south to reach Taba, which is designed to become a retail and entertainment magnet for this stretch of shoreline.

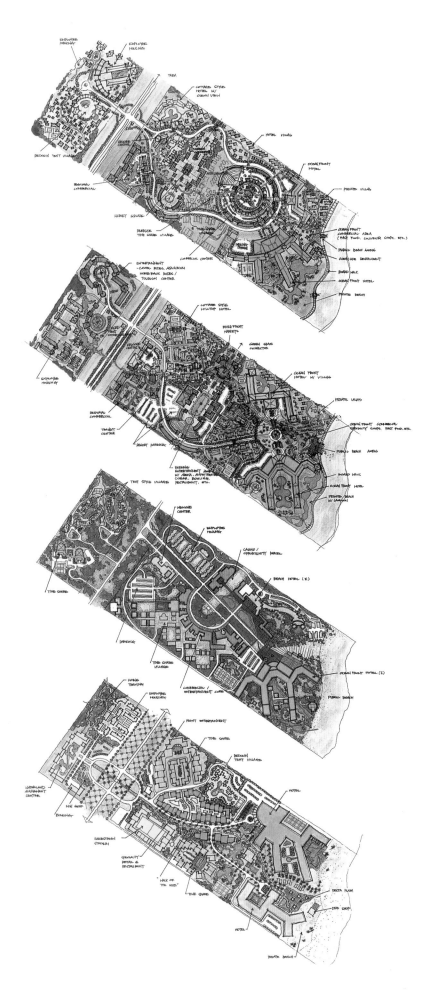

1

Imagery:

1 Early concept options
2 Malawi resort villas
3 Luxor square arcade
4 Land-use plan
5 Festival park
6 Thebes village retail
7 Master plan

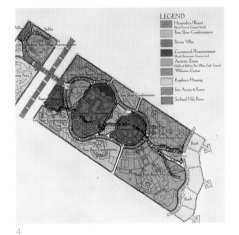

Taruma Resort

Design/Completion: 1993/under construction
Bogor, Republic of Indonesia
PT Pasir Wangun
3,488 acres/1,412 hectares

The plan for Taruma, a resort community in Bogor, is a good example of how design and planning can take advantage of natural surroundings. Residences in a variety of styles near the site's center adapt to the hilly terrain, and take advantage of the stunning backdrop of Mt Salak, an active volcano. Residential streets, aligned along terraces, create a village reminiscent of an ancient Greek hill town. Single-family villas are planned for the higher terrain overlooking stream valleys, creating water views while leaving the streams intact. Existing hot springs enhance the gathering-place appeal of a spa, a community center with a mosque, and an amphitheater. The design concept preserves and connects natural greenspaces throughout the site. Jogging and biking paths give residents access to the greenspaces as well as to all other community amenities.

A distinct feature of the design draws its inspiration from the well-known Bogor botanical gardens. A promenade, arcing through the center of the site, is designed to be a botanical garden of its own, richly landscaped with indigenous tropical plants. The promenade provides a dramatic focal point to the site. It leads to a teahouse near the hill town, with views of Jakarta to the north.

Future phases of the Taruma plan will add two 18-hole golf courses, an equestrian center, and rail access for visitors from Jakarta.

Pacific Coast Builders Conference Gold Nugget Award – Merit Award, Best New Town Plan, 1994

1

2

3

4

Imagery:
1   Hotel pool illustration
2   Village center aerial
3   Hillside villas
4   Mount Salak
5   Lighthouse point
    illustration
6   Master plan

5

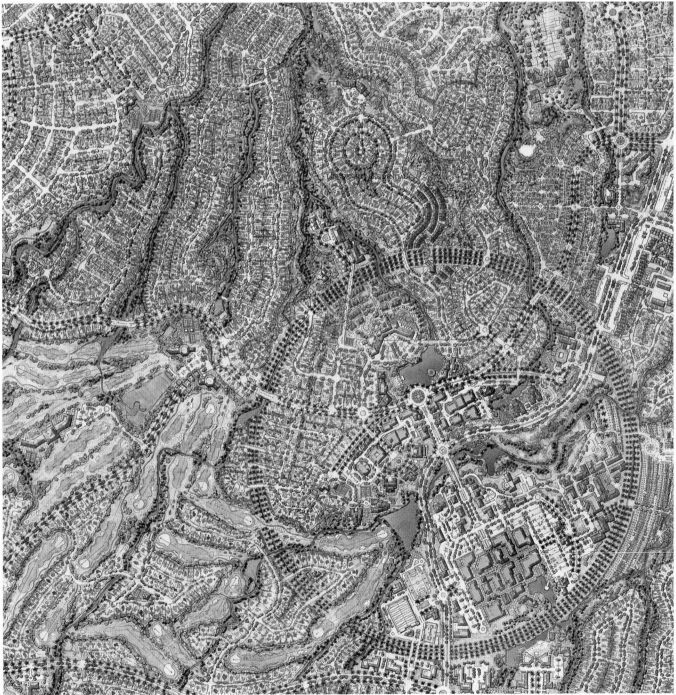

6

Telaga Kahuripan

Design/Completion: 1995/under
construction
Parung, Republic of Indonesia
PT Kahuripan Raya
1,734 acres/702 hectares

Telaga Kahuripan, a residential development within commuting distance of Jakarta, adapts to its location, on the site of a former rubber plantation, in ways that not only create minimal disruption to the local rubber industry, but also use the plantation as a key design asset. Rather than remove the rubber trees, planners oriented Telaga's neighborhoods and Dutch Colonial residences around them, using their shape, beauty, and shade to create greenspace common areas for the shared use of residents.

Telaga transforms other natural features into design assets, also. The entry road ends at a striking Dutch Colonial entry gate beside the site's most prominent lake. Development along a central spine preserves existing terraced rice paddies, and integrates nature walks and jogging paths among them. Housing follows the Indonesian 1:3:6 formula: for every one low-density unit there are three of medium density and six of high density. Neighborhoods, village centers, nature preserves, an 18-hole golf course, and a resort hotel are arranged around existing freshwater lakes, giving residents lake views and easy access to swimming and boating. One notable design feature is a waterfall that starts at a courtyard fountain behind a lakeside clubhouse, cascades through the center of the building beneath a glass-block lobby floor, and continues down a series of landscaped terraces to the lake.

Telaga is designed as a first-home community, with business parks, schools, and neighborhood centers complementing retail, entertainment, and recreational amenities.

Imagery:
1 Poolside at golf clubhouse
2 Monumental gateway
3 Feature cascade lake
Opposite Master plan

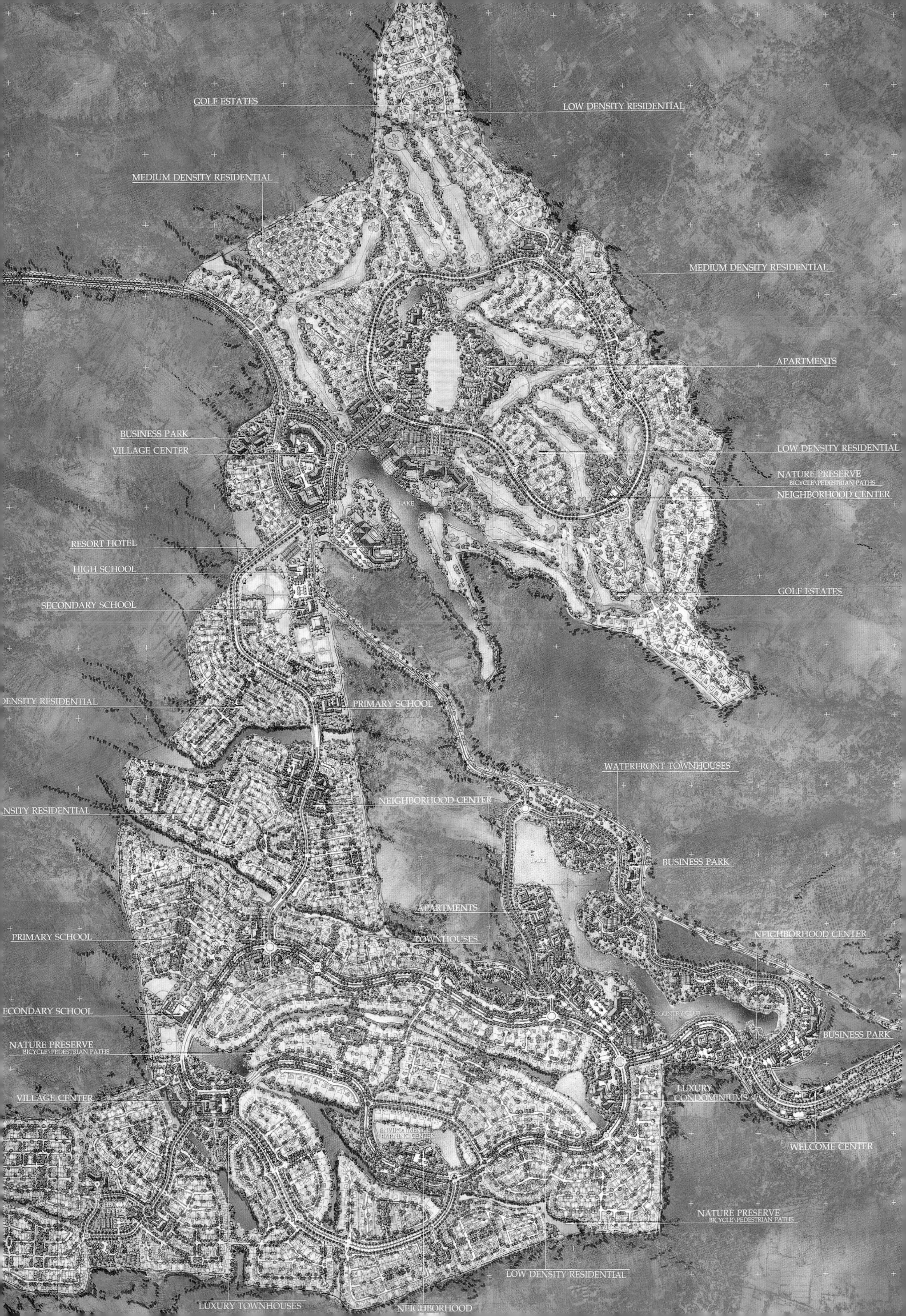
GOLF ESTATES
LOW DENSITY RESIDENTIAL
MEDIUM DENSITY RESIDENTIAL
MEDIUM DENSITY RESIDENTIAL
APARTMENTS
BUSINESS PARK
VILLAGE CENTER
LOW DENSITY RESIDENTIAL
NATURE PRESERVE
BICYCLE\PEDESTRIAN PATHS
NEIGHBORHOOD CENTER
LAKE
RESORT HOTEL
HIGH SCHOOL
SECONDARY SCHOOL
GOLF ESTATES
DENSITY RESIDENTIAL
PRIMARY SCHOOL
WATERFRONT TOWNHOUSES
NEIGHBORHOOD CENTER
NSITY RESIDENTIAL
LAKE
BUSINESS PARK
APARTMENTS
TOWNHOUSES
PRIMARY SCHOOL
NEIGHBORHOOD CENTER
ECONDARY SCHOOL
COUNTRY CLUB
BUSINESS PARK
NATURE PRESERVE
BICYCLE\PEDESTRIAN PATHS
VILLAGE CENTER
LUXURY
CONDOMINIUMS
WELCOME CENTER
NATURE PRESERVE
BICYCLE\PEDESTRIAN PATHS
LOW DENSITY RESIDENTIAL
LUXURY TOWNHOUSES
NEIGHBORHOOD

5

6

7

8

9

10

11

Zonk'izizwe Master Plan

Design/Completion: 1996/on-going
Midrand, Gauteng, Republic of South Africa
Old Mutual Properties
Land area: 375 acres/152 hectares
Building area: 5,000,000 square feet/
464,684 square meters

1

Imagery:
1 Gondola sketch
2 Site plan
3 Festival plaza
4 Mall atrium
5 Courtyard sketch
6 Promenade section
7 Concept model
   aerial

A distinctive, curvilinear shape defines the core of Zonk'izizwe, a design for a shopping and entertainment resort between Johannesburg and Pretoria, and gives it an unmistakably African imprint. Two wings that arc from a center plaza and curve as though to embrace a lakefront, borrow their shape from the horns of the water buffalo, which is indigenous to this part of Africa. More generally, throughout Sub-Saharan Africa it is curving forms that define villages and communities, in contrast to the sharp, rectangular grid plans of European towns.

Zonk'izizwe, which means "all nations," celebrates its African heritage and climate with open-air pedestrian streets, and an orientation that allows the winter sun to warm its terraces and public spaces. On islands in an artificial lake are an aquarium, adventure tours, and towers for views of the surrounding region. Bridges from the center island (including one marked by a "discovery tower") go to a lakefront promenade, which connects to a central plaza with bright African paving designs. At the center is a central marketplace rotunda;

the "horns" are open promenades linking the plaza and rotunda to department stores and other commercial establishments. To the north is an entertainment district with a multi-screen cinema complex; to the south is an arts and crafts center. Resort hotels are north and south of the lake. The plan also provides for integrated town homes and office uses. The entire resort is family oriented, combining interactive learning, recreation, shopping, dining, and entertainment.

2

3

4

5

7

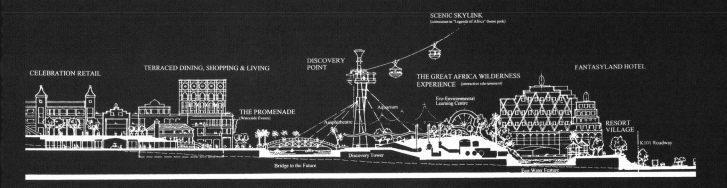

SCENIC SKYLINK
(connection to "Legends of Africa" theme park)

DISCOVERY
POINT

FANTASYLAND HOTEL

CELEBRATION RETAIL

TERRACED DINING, SHOPPING & LIVING

THE GREAT AFRICA WILDERNESS
EXPERIENCE (interactive edu-tainment)

Eco-Environmental
Learning Centre

THE PROMENADE
(Waterside Events)

Aquarium

Amphitheatre

RESORT
VILLAGE

K101 Roadway

Bridge to the Future

Discovery Tower

Eco-Water Feature

6

HOLIDAY INN BALI HAI

PRIVATE COUNTRY RESIDENCE

PRIVATE PENTHOUSE RESIDENCE

PLAZA YOGYA

MARBELLA RESIDENCIA

MARRIOTT INTERNATIONAL

RADISSON PLAZA SUITES

PARK ROYAL

GOLF VIEW TERRACES

KAPUK GOLF CLUBHOUSE

VIZCAYA AT DUNE ALLEN

HOSPITALITY

Holiday Inn Bali Hai Resort

Design/Completion: 1991/1993
Bali, Republic of Indonesia
Okason Group/PT Bank Dagang Bali
137,730 square feet/12,800 square meters
Concrete and masonry
Lcal stone, brick and timber

Traditional Balinese architecture and culture were the driving forces in the design of this 192-room Holiday Inn resort, located on Kuta Bay. The strong cultural influences are evident at the point of entry, revealed in a Balinese temple situated off the hotel reception area, at the highest point in the complex. The temple overlooks the pool, which is surrounded by stone-and-stucco hotel units with their ornately designed tile roofs, and thatch-roofed pavilions reminiscent of Balinese sleeping huts. Many cottages include prayer shrines for guests,

fabric designs use traditional patterns, and rich landscaping with integrated water features and bright floral colors reflect the Hindu influence on the island.

Bali Hai showcases the handiwork of the local artisans and craftspeople who carved the stone friezes and sculptures throughout the resort, built prayer towers and furniture for the grounds, and helped construct the highly detailed, stone mosaic foundations undergirding the bridges and buildings built over and on canals and ponds in the resort. Accommodations range from single rooms to four-unit, walled garden villas. Hotel amenities include a restaurant with an outdoor dining terrace, a poolside grill and water bar, retail shops, a health club, and a nightclub.

Imagery: 1   Pool terrace
          2   Morning at Bali Hai

1

3

4

5

6

7

8

Private Country Residence

Design/Completion: 1997/1998
Baltimore, MD, USA
Undisclosed
5,400 square feet/501 square meters

Mediterranean vernacular styles strongly influence this eclectic home, located on a rural hillside north of Baltimore. Its three sections, in a U-shaped layout, create the sense of a series of farm buildings that have been linked over time, and its three-foot-thick walls are of rough-cut stone, like old farmhouses found on Southern French and Italian hillsides. in order to promote light and ventilation, no section is more than one room deep.

Inside, exposed chestnut beams, a wood-plank ceiling, and distressed, random-width walnut flooring enhance the aged-farmhouse effect. Ceiling heights vary from 2.5 to 4 meters (8–13 feet); hallways are intentionally narrow. Both features add variety as one moves through the house. All windows and doors are of the double French-door style. Window openings widen toward the interior, to bring in more light. The house has five bedrooms, plus a guest apartment above the garage, accessible by a circular stair within a tower.

The house and the site encourage outdoor activity. An up-slope stand of trees, and a

Imagery:

1	Dining room
2	Living room
3	Main gate
4	Entry in winter
5	Loggia entry
6	Wine cellar
7	Loggia
8	Pool
9	Kitchen
Following pages	Evening vista

foundation cut into the hillside offer protection from wind. The house's southern orientation brings light, warmth, and pleasing views of the valley below. A pool and loggia create an outdoor "room" where the owners can enjoy the natural surroundings.

9

5

6

8

7

Private Penthouse Residence

Design/Completion: 1991/1994
Istanbul, Turkey
Client undisclosed
16,140 square feet/1,500 square meters
Exotic woods, stones, ceramics, custom
ironwork

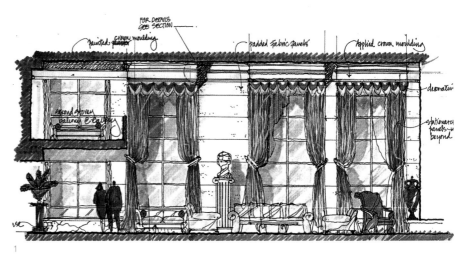

A majestic entryway sets the tone for this penthouse residence, located on the top two floors of a 23-story Istanbul residential tower. After arriving by elevator at the upper level, one descends from the foyer down a grand marble stairway. The stairway narrows between stone walls to highlight the entrance to the main-floor living area, with its panoramic view of Istanbul harbor and the Bosphorus Strait to the southeast. An upper-level balcony overlooks the living area, and a stone fireplace marks its apex. A rustic wine court is behind the base of the stairway.

Down one wing are kitchen and dining areas, servants' quarters, and a bedroom suite; down the other are an entertainment den and another bedroom suite. Master suites on the second level are adjacent to a skylit court with a pool equipped for stationary swimming.

The V-shaped luxury apartment is designed in the style of a 15th century Italian villa, with abundant stone, and other rich materials and textures throughout. It is furnished with

custom-designed furniture and light fixtures, and an eclectic array of antiques selected by the owner on travels around the world.

Imagery:
1 Living room, south wall elevation
2 Formal living room illustration

1

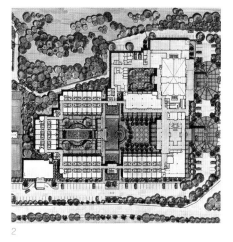

2

Design/Completion: 1992/1995
Yogyakarta, Republic of Indonesia
Salim Group
163,164 square feet/15,164 square meters
Reinforced concrete frame
Masonry with plaster façade, wood/heavy
timber accents

Imagery: 1   Main lobby
           2   Site plan
           3   Porte-cochere
           4   Overall elevation

A Dutch Colonial architectural style is well
suited to this 200-room luxury hotel, which
attracts an international mix of travelers
drawn to the historic Borobudur temple and
other landmarks of Yogyakarta's past. Set in
the mountains of Java, in a region rich in the
ruins and artifacts of ancient Javanese
civilization, the city is a former Dutch
protectorate, and served briefly as
Indonesia's capital in the mid-1900s.

Two main courtyards help define the various
moods of the hotel. One, a tree-lined open
plaza directly behind the main reception
area, and adjacent to a central fountain and
swimming pool, is an area of high activity.
The other, richly landscaped with trees,
shrubs, and indigenous flowers, is more
serene. Banquet facilities, shops, and a
health club are among other hotel amenities.

In elevation, the lines of the rooftops and
towers integrate with window arches and
arched passageways to create an elegant
symmetry. Red-tile roofs and thick walls
finished with white-washed stucco fit the
vernacular style. Hotel rooms have dark,
random-wood floors and high ceilings with
ceiling fans, to keep rooms cool in the
tropical climate.

3

4

Marbella Residencia

Design/Completion: 1993/1995
Anyer, Java, Republic of Indonesia
PT Pudjiadi Prestige, Ltd
1,291,200 square feet/120,000 square meters
Reinforced concrete
Stucco-rendered brick, clay tile roof, local hardwoods

1

Marbella Residencia borrows its name and architectural inspiration from a small village in Spain which has a central courtyard plaza as its centerpiece. Like its namesake, the focal point of this 1,300-unit, beachfront condominium community is a central courtyard, which features cobblestone plazas, rich landscaping, ponds filled with fish and water plants, and a swimming pool. The stone and stucco, red-tile roofs, heavy wooden beams, and prominent wrought iron features throughout the development also reflect the Mediterranean influence of southern Spain.

Marbella has four building clusters of about 325 units, each set in a "U" shape around the pool courtyard. Units range from efficiency apartments to three-bedroom suites, each with an outdoor terrace. All units are set at an angle to create views of the Sunda Strait, connecting the Java Sea and the Indian Ocean on Java's eastern tip. What remains of the Krakatoa volcano is also visible from Marbella. The building height steps down to create a more human scale closer to the pool and beach. The varying building heights also increase the number of penthouse apartments in the complex.

Imagery:
1 Swimming pool
2 Residential courtyard
3 Site plan

2

3

6

7

8

Marriott Hotels

Various locations
Marriott International, Washington, DC

Marriott International is one of Design Group's steady clients in the hospitality industry. The firm has completed facelifts for existing hotels showing signs of age, and has helped design entry points, public areas, reception facilities, and lounges and bars for Marriott. Design Group has also been instrumental in shaping the interior design of Marriott's popular Courtyard hotels in the USA and Europe. In its latest venture, the firm is working to create prototypes for new hotel brands Marriott plans to introduce early in the 21st century.

Imagery:
1 Study model, Way Halim, Sumatra, Indonesia
2 Lobby, Tyson's Corner, McClean, Virginia, USA
3 Sample board, MVCI Legend's Edge, Bay Point, Florida, USA
4 Sample board, Tyson's Corner, McClean, Virginia, USA
5 Lounge, Galeria Glodok, Jakarta, Indonesia

6 Lobby elevation, Galeria Glodok, Jakarta, Indonesia
7 Galeria Glodok, Jakarta, Indonesia
Background Ground floor plan, San Francisco, California, USA

1

2

Radisson Plaza Suite Hotel

Design/Completion: 1992/1994
Surabaya, Republic of Indonesia
PT Bayu Beringin Lestari/PT Indomarco
Nusatrada
Existing reinforced concrete structure
Pre-cast panel, marble, glass skylight

1

The Radisson Plaza Suite in Surabaya, Indonesia's second-largest city, is an inventive example of adaptive re-use, involving the conversion of a former seven-story parking garage into a 240-room, all-suite luxury hotel with space and amenities for business conferences. The floor-to-floor heights of the parking garage, though incompatible with office space or other uses, were adaptable for hospitality use.

The key to the conversion was addition by subtraction. Design Group eliminated two circular auto ramps at either end of what had

been an imposing rectangular structure, and cut out its center—in effect creating two buildings. A skylit glass atrium running the full height of the structure connects the two new halves, with an atrium lobby at ground level and connecting footbridges at every floor above. From the upper floors visitors have eye-catching views down into the lobby, where trees and other plantings surround the dining area of a first-floor restaurant. Tall banner graphics and distinctive elevator lifts draw attention to the skylight, and promote movement between

floors. The interior courtyard is finished stone with a marble floor and marble wall accents. Rooms in the Radisson are oriented inward, with balconies extending out into the atrium.

Imagery:
1 Skylight at main entry
2 Atrium restaurant
3 Lobby/coffee lounge
4 Main entry
5 Reception hall

3

2

4

5

Park Royal

Design/Completion: 1994/1997
Jakarta, Republic of Indonesia
PT Slipi Sri Indopuri
267,752 square feet/24,884 square meters
Hotel: 195 keys; Apartment complex: 64 units
Reinforced concrete frame
Pre-cast concrete accents, tinted glass panels

2

3

4

Park Royal, a 24-story hotel and serviced-apartment complex, creates a place of residential calm in the middle of Indonesia's busiest city. An L-shaped apartment tower and a hotel tower are oriented inward, away from the noise and congestion of Jakarta's streets, focusing instead on a central, three-tiered interior courtyard.

At the ground level, a single porte-cochère is the entry point for both towers, with walkways leading to lobbies and lounges. (Apartment residents can also enter directly through a parking garage.) A serpentine, glass-enclosed walkway at the back of the porte-cochère also connects the towers, and marks the rise in elevation to the next tier, a palm-lined pool area. At its back edge is another curving, glass-enclosed walkway, taking its shape from the curve of the back of the pool. This marks the rise to the third tier, a greenspace and park with jogging paths and other recreational amenities. A park-level fountain cascades over the walkway into the pool. Each successive rise is further removed from the noise of the street.

The towers are positioned to bring sunlight into the complex's interior and into inward-facing rooms, most of which have glass fronts across their main living areas. The heavily serrated, inward-facing side of the hotel creates a maximum number of highly desired corner rooms.

Imagery: 1 Overview
2 Site plan
3 Project section
4 Residential tower lobby

Golf View Terraces

Design/Completion: 1991/1996
Jakarta, Republic of Indonesia
Brasali Realty
452,318 square feet/42,0137 square meters
Reinforced concrete
Stone and stucco

Golf View Terraces makes imaginative use of a small site to create a 200-unit, luxury condominium complex which gives each resident a view of the Pondok Indah golf course. A V-shaped design opening out toward the course, and heavily serrated towers that create more corner views are the keys to creating the necessary sight lines. Golf View Terraces is well named; outdoor terraces for each apartment also have golf-course views.

Another challenge was to create a complex of this size on a small site, located in a region with strict building height regulations. Designers resolved this problem by breaking the complex into two identical towers in close proximity with each other. The towers share a common porte-cochère and fountain courtyard, as well as a garden, a pool, tennis courts, a jogging trail, and other amenities. A covered walkway connects the towers at the ground level. A grand stone stairway marks the transition from the arrival location to the pool and garden.

The complex's one-, two-, and three-bedroom luxury apartments all have trademark octagonal entry foyers. Paving patterns in granite and limestone, and intricate tile designs are among its other design features.

Imagery:
1 View from garden walkway
2 Site plan
3 Overall project illustration
Opposite West building from pool plaza

1

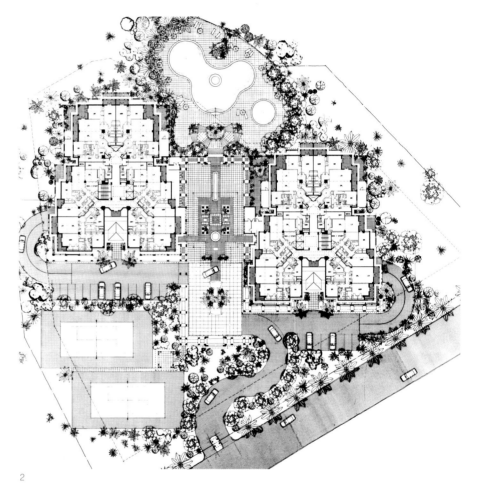

2

3

5

Imagery: 5   View from Pondok
                Indah golf course
           6   West building
                elevation
           7   East building from
                pool terrace
           8   Elevator lobby

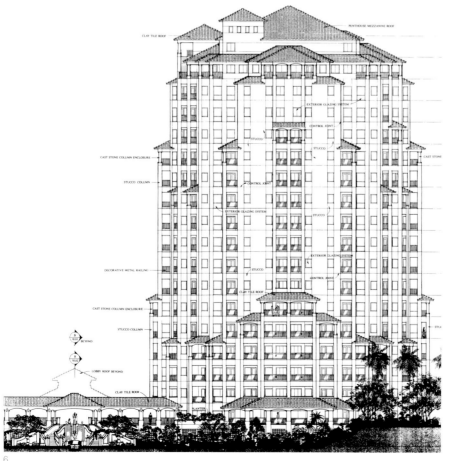

6

Pantai Indah Kapuk Golf Clubhouse

Design/Completion: 1989/1991
Jakarta, Republic of Indonesia
PT Mandara Permai
61,290 square feet/5,696 square meters
Concrete frame building, wood frame roof
Cooper roof, stone cladding, hardwoods
and granite floor

The distinctive curved form of the Pantai Indah Kapuk Golf Clubhouse, built on the site of former shrimp and fish farms near the Java Sea, maximizes the panoramic view of the adjacent golf course in ways that a more conventional rectilinear shape could not. This form dictated a complex and inventive design for the clubhouse, with rooms widening toward the outer edge of the arc facing the golf course, a championship course designed by Robert Trent Jones, Jr.

The clubhouse combines subtle beauty and simple, functional elegance. Visitors arrive at an oval porte-cochère marked by a fountain at the arc's center. As they move into the clubhouse, its curved form creates the panorama. Battered stone walls support a gently sloping, green copper roof. Large roof overhangs help the structure blend with the landscape, and provide relief from Indonesia's at-times intense heat. A cathedral ceiling showcases an intricate indigenous wood-slat design done in native teak. The building's design and siting allow cooling breezes to filter through the open-air restaurant and terrace. A gracefully arching,

1

stone footbridge crosses a pond to connect the clubhouse terrace to the golf course. The wood, stone, and metal used in construction are all from the region.

Planned future phases of the project will create a swimming and tennis clubhouse along a west side extension of the arc.

Imagery: 1   Main entry
            2   Site plan
            3   View from golf
                course

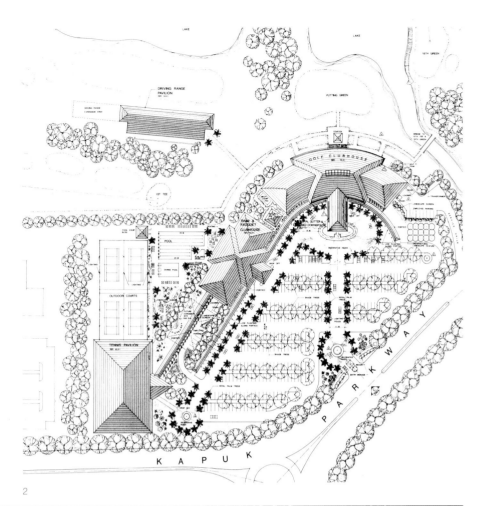

2

3

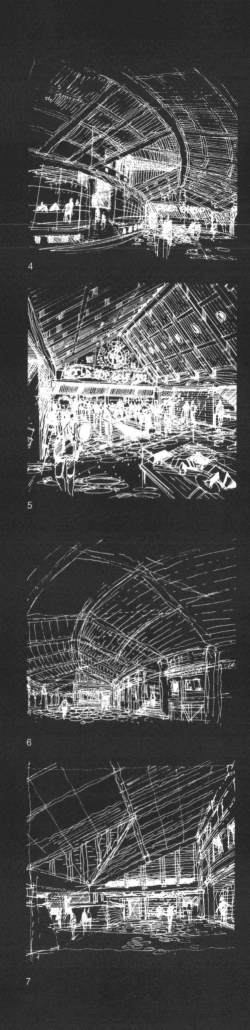

4

5

6

7

8

Imagery: 4–7   Early concept
                        sketches
            8   View from entry road
            9   Kapuk clubhouse
          10   Main dining room

9

10

Vizcaya at Dune Allen

Design/Completion: 1990/1999
Walton County, Florida, USA
The Howard Group
12 acres/4 hectares
Wood frames
Stucco façade, clay tile roof, wood timber
accents

A consistent architectural theme used
throughout Vizcaya at Dune Allen creates a
Mediterranean-style coastal village on the
Florida panhandle. The Mediterranean
transition begins along a tree-lined entry
drive that leads to a gated entrance marked
by two towers, and flanked by garden walls
and cypress trees. Inside, the richly
landscaped community of two- and three-
story single-family homes offers variations on
the Mediterranean theme, with stucco siding
and red-tile roofs, tall chimneys that break up
the skyline, bell towers, wrought-iron gates
and ornamentation, streets lined with gas
lamps, and hand-painted tile accents.
Residents share a common pool and plaza.
Streets are staggered to give each house a
view of the beach.

Environmental factors figured heavily in the
design. Design Group worked closely with
federal officials to ensure only minimal
disruption to sand dunes, indigenous
vegetation, and a nearby nesting habitat for
turtles. A concern both during construction
and afterward was the threat of hurricanes,
which are common in the region. Vizcaya has
withstood several since the first units were
built.

As the community grows, maintaining the
design vernacular will be critical. In order to
guarantee long-term design integrity, Design
Group worked with local officials and
residents to write building covenants that
allow growth only within specific design
parameters.

Imagery: 1   Gulf-view residences
             2   Community
                  streetscape
             3   Building details
             4   Gulf-view residences
             5   Site plan
          Below   Project entry

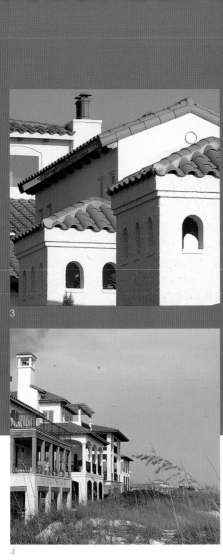

3

4

2

5

FIRM PROFILE

DEVELOPMENT
DESIGN
GROUP
INCORPORATED

Development Design Group, Inc.

Development Design Group, Inc. is one of the largest architecture and planning practices in Maryland. From our Baltimore headquarters, the firm's multi-disciplinary, multi-lingual teams design high-profile, award-winning international destinations, including themed retail, entertainment, leisure, town centers, hospitality, resort, residential, commercial, and mixed-use developments.

left to right: Michial Alston, Ahsin Rasheed, Jim Andreone, Roy Higgs, John Clark, Pipat Esara, Ana Ruthie Galang, Valerie Knauff

Roy H. Higgs

Chief Executive Officer

One of many odd jobs Roy Higgs had growing up in post-World War II England was driving a truck that that delivered armaments to the Tower of London. In order to make the deliveries, Higgs, who at the time had no previous experience in driving trucks, had to pass under an archway that was just barely higher and wider than the truck itself. On some occasions his aim was less than perfect, and he would scrape through, terrorizing the British Beefeater guarding the entrance and taking divots of stone and concrete from the arch. Years later, while on a trip to Europe, he would show off these scars to his family. The story may be somewhat of a metaphor for Higgs's career, since it marks his earliest confrontation with a recognized architectural landmark.

Colleagues sometimes call Higgs the 'anti-architect'. Though not entirely accurate, the label reflects his frustration with many of what have come to be regarded as fine architectural monuments, but which Higgs finds lacking in their ability to meet the needs

of those who must use them. And the label comes from his advocacy of a style of architecture that removes the design of buildings and places from the exclusive domain of trained, professional architects and places it at the center of a more organic process that involves owners, users, and other stakeholders, and gives careful consideration to a design's cultural context.

Higgs's own professional training in architecture and design was less than conventional. Some early formal study of art and industrial design helped him build upon his natural talent for drawing, but he was impatient with school, and got most of his education on the job. The big break of his career came in his teens, when he was hired to undertake store design for a company in London that made store fixtures. There Higgs was given the freedom to try new things, learn from his mistakes, and generally to flex his creative muscles.

Higgs left England and set off to see the world, supporting himself by drawing for architectural firms and doing freelance design of stores and restaurants. He had worked his way through Europe to South Africa when he met the woman he would marry, and they settled in Johannesburg. He took a job there in the regional office of Design International, a design firm headquartered in Toronto, Canada, then later relocated to the United States to open the firm's newest branch. Higgs met and hired partner-to-be John Clark, and the two grew the firm into the quasi-independent DI Architecture. In 1993, DI Architecture became the fully independent Development Design Group.

As Design Group's CEO, Higgs oversees the design and execution of retail, entertainment, hospitality, office, residential, and mixed-use projects of every imaginable scale, in every corner of the globe. He continues to have very much of a hands-on influence on the firm's work. Among the many projects that bear his imprint are the Zonk'izizwe master plan in South Africa, the plan for Toronto's Cornell Town Centre, Pretoria's Menlyn Park, Johannesburg's The Zone@Rosebank, and Robertson Walk in Singapore.

Higgs's nearly twenty years with the firm have been immensely satisfying. Under his leadership, Design Group has weathered two major recessions, launched a hugely successful venture into international design

that now finds it undertaking work for clients on five continents, garnered a passel of awards, and earned a reputation as one of the world's top international architecture and design firms.

One of the chief reasons for the Design Group's international success has been its focus on bringing in new and diverse talent from around the globe, and its eighty-five designers from more than twenty countries are testament to the success of that endeavor. But Higgs's interest in cultivating new talent goes beyond the firm's needs. Knowing first-hand how important it is to have someone put their confidence in you and give you a break early in your career, he developed an internship program that brings promising young designers from developing countries and disadvantaged backgrounds to Design Group for an extended stay. Afterward the interns take their growing skills and experience back to their home country and play a role in its ongoing development. The program has been a great success.

Higgs is a frequent speaker at international conferences on design and commercial development, and serves as an awards juror for architectural, retail, and planning associations. He is a regular contributor to industry periodicals and a member of the architecture and design editorial board of the journal Shopping Center Business. He is active in a range of professional associations, including the American Planning Association, the Institute of Store Planners, the International Real Estate Federation (FIABCI), the Urban Land Institute, and the International Council of Shopping Centers. In 1997, Higgs and Clark were named co-recipients of the Maryland State Award for International Business Leadership.

By combining architectural skill and design creativity with a sharp business sense, John Clark has helped reshape many conventional notions about commercial design and development. A prime example of Clark's penchant for innovation can be seen in the attention he and Design Group give to merchandizing during the early phases of a project. Where some firms would design and build a commercial center and then fill it with whichever tenants were willing to lease it, Clark begins with a leasing plan that ensures an optimum tenant mix, and the strength of that plan has a major influence on a center's success.

Clark, whose career took a brief but not unrelated detour into the restaurant business in the mid-1970s, has had a pioneering impact in other areas as well. He is a staunch advocate of retail theming—of using architecture to create themes tied to a particular place, such as ancient Egypt or small-town America, or to an activity such as golf or sailing. Where conventional wisdom once held that no retail complex could survive without a department store anchor, Clark has successfully introduced un-anchored or unconventionally anchored retail centers, adding entertainment venues and other elements to attract business. These concepts are on display in his design for Cocowalk, in Coconut Grove, Florida, which integrated restaurants, cinema, and other entertainment experiences with retail shopping in order to help create the genre known today as the 'urban entertainment center'.

As the unconventional proves its worth, it in turn becomes the new convention. It is hard to recall a time when the food court was not standard in every suburban shopping mall. Outlet centers with recognizable, upscale merchants offering goods at off-market prices have joined their lower-budget counterparts on the retail landscape. Bold graphics and other environmental elements, and open-air shopping and dining have become commonplace. But there was a time when all of these were groundbreaking ideas, and Clark was among the first take up the conceptual pick and shovel.

One thing contributing towards Clark's knack for innovation is that at the age of 56 he is one of the more senior members of the American baby-boom generation that has had such a sweeping influence on global commercial culture, and who collectively are the single most influential users of the places Design Group creates. Whether it is a desire for a place of calm in a world grown hectic, a craving for more rewarding leisure-time activities, or a quest for the perfect spot for a family outing, Clark has been able to predict the kind of place or experience baby boomers want a step before they realize they want it. That awareness is likely to continue to influence Design Group's work as more boomers reach retirement age.

The design of retail and entertainment destinations remains Clark's forte. His designs show special sensitivity to their setting, and strive for a distinctive identity that evokes a sense of place. Clark's work also shows the influence of his frequent travels throughout Europe, South America, and Asia, and in particular his affinity for the architecture and ambience of small villages around the Mediterranean Sea. In addition to Cocowalk, Clark's recent projects include the Centro Ybor night-time entertainment destination near Tampa, Florida; Easton Town Center, a neo-traditional community in Columbus, Ohio; Newport on the Levee, near Cincinnati; and designs for several of Muvico Theaters' cinema complexes.

As president of Design Group, Clark coordinates the development of new business and oversees concept development and design direction for many of the firm's architectural commissions.

John B. Clark, R.A.

President

Ahsin Rasheed, APA, R.A.

Senior Vice President
Director of Planning

You expect someone in charge of master planning to be a big-picture person, and without a doubt, Ahsin Rasheed's achievements go beyond the measure. After joining Design Group in 1987, he initially found himself concentrating on the design of shopping centers and retail environments. But circumstances soon guided him into a planning role, which he relished. Among Rasheed's earliest projects were a mixed-use waterfront development plan in Scotland, known as Edinburgh Maritime, and a plan for the commercial core of Kentlands, a neo-traditional community near Washington, DC. These projects were his first steps toward becoming Design Group's director of planning.

Ahsin Rasheed's career path began to take shape very early in his life, when as a child growing up in Pakistan he spent time watching designers, architects, planners, and engineers in the offices of his father, a transportation planner. Primarily attracted to the design side of the business, he went on to study architecture in Lahore, and then completed his undergraduate education in the United States, earning a bachelor degree in 1983. It was during this time that he began to develop a strong interest in large-scale planning, and after a brief stint working in Pakistan, he returned to the United States to undertake the graduate studies in Minnesota that would eventually support this growing interest.

The satisfaction Rasheed gets from his work comes from considering an extraordinarily wide range of variables—economic and social issues, cultural considerations, demographics, environmental concerns, and geography, to name a few—and bringing them into equilibrium in the design of a built environment that meets real human needs. The design solution—the synthesis—cannot be arrived at simply by feeding data into a computer, applying a formula, and waiting for a result. Large-scale planning requires a creative blend of science, art, and intuition, and Rasheed has built his career by being successful at it.

Under Rasheed's direction, master planning has become a central part of Design Group's work, and the firm's planning portfolio has grown substantially. Taking the broad view, but also minding the details, Rasheed has integrated a planner's perspective into Design Group projects ranging in size from ten hectares to ten thousand, in Asia, Africa, and North America. In the process he has helped the firm win numerous design awards, including several Pacific Coast Builders' Conference Gold Nugget awards for new town planning (for Pantai Indah Kapuk, Kota Legenda, Taman Impian Jaya Ancol' and Taruma Resort to name a few). Dreamland in Cairo; Pantai Kapuknaga and Telaga Kahuripan in Indonesia; and the urban revitalization plan for downtown Johannesburg in South Africa are among the many master plans he has created for Design Group.

Vice President

James Andreone's broad experience in virtually every phase of every kind of architectural project is what makes him ideally suited to managing many of Design Group's most complicated and challenging projects. Though his earliest experience with design was building a tree house in his backyard while growing up in Baltimore, his career in architecture began in the late 1970s. After a brief period as a science teacher, he returned to study architecture, and later got a job as a student intern in Baltimore with RTKL. That position led to full-time work as an RTKL project architect and designer, and his involvement in a wide range of retail, residential, and hospital designs. Later, with another Baltimore firm, Andreone gained invaluable experience with larger and more complex projects, such as the mixed-use Colonnade condominium and hotel complex in downtown Baltimore and the 60,000 square meter Skyway Metro Center retail mall in New York City.

Andreone, who has a degree in architecture from the University of Maryland, joined Design Group as a project architect in 1993, attracted by the firm's growing portfolio of international projects. One of the most rewarding and educational of these was the Tunjungan Plaza hotel and mall, a renovation and expansion project that created what is perhaps the largest retail building in all of Indonesia. The project was satisfying, not only because of the challenge of integrating new designs with existing components, but also because it gave Andreone insight into the need to be sensitive to cultural differences when carrying out a project. Other international projects he has directed include Marbella Residencia, Park Royal, and the Radisson Surabaya. Reflecting his penchant for tackling a challenge, he is also heavily involved in Design Group's work for Muvico Theaters, one of the firm's most progressive clients.

Michial C. Alston, R.A.

Vice President

The kinds of projects Michial Alston finds most attractive are those where the client does not know exactly what they want beyond the fact that no one has ever done it before. That was the mindset behind two projects that have been especially significant in shaping Alston's career: Cocowalk, Design Group's genre-creating urban entertainment center, and Easton Town Center, the award-winning "new old town" that has made a significant contribution to the New Urbanism school of community design. Alston worked closely with company president John Clark on both projects.

Alston, who comes from a small farming community in North Carolina, never envisioned a career as a principal with a major international architecture firm when he started on his career path. As a boy he loved to draw, and he was attracted to architecture because someone told him that that was all architects did! He studied architecture at Virginia Polytechnic Institute and State University, and at the university's extension program at the Washington-Alexandria Center for Architecture, near the nation's capital. His first job after graduating was undertaking institutional design for Probst-Mason, a Baltimore firm. From there, he went to the Columbia Design Collective, and joined Design Group (then DI Architecture) in 1987.

Alston may have begun his career because he thought all architects did was draw, but his broad experience has taught him that there's more to it than that. His work with Design Group has taken him from the farming town of his youth to the management of projects in Singapore, Hong Kong, China, Europe, and the Caribbean. In the process he has learned the nuances of working in countries that are very different politically, economically, and culturally from the United States. Today, in addition to overseeing project design, Alston is involved in marketing and general operations, and serves as a client liaison point. He is also a licensed electrician, and enjoys designing and building lighting fixtures as a hobby.

Director of Hospitality
Allied Member, ASID
Senior Associate

Sometimes a designer might dream of working on a project where cost is—if not irrelevant—at least not a major consideration. That dream was a reality, briefly, for Ruth Galang in the early 1990s, when she outfitted palaces, villas, and penthouse apartments with silk wall coverings, custom-designed rugs, antique furniture, and other luxuries as an interior designer with CADO, a firm near Washington, DC. But what gives Design Group's hospitality director more satisfaction is working within very real budget constraints to create an interior space that pleases the client, works for the user, and is aesthetically satisfying.

Born and raised in the Philippines, Galang was heavily influenced in her career choice by her two older sisters, one trained as an interior designer and the other as an architect. (Both would eventually work for Design Group.) Following their lead and wanting an outlet for her own creative talents, Galang studied fine arts at the University of Santo Tomas in the Philippines, earning a bachelor's degree in 1974. After working briefly as an ad designer for a graphic design firm, she moved to the United States, and took a job as a junior interior designer with Marriott International, Inc. She joined Design Group in 1996.

Galang's twenty years of experience in design—including fifteen in hospitality—leave her well positioned to run Design Group's hospitality division. She handles marketing and client relations, and oversees designs and project management for all of the firm's interior design projects. Because Design Group does a substantial amount of work for Marriott, Galang maintains a close relationship with her former employer. Among the many projects she has overseen are Marriott Courtyard hotels (Eaton Centre) in Toronto, Canada; in San Antonio (River Center), Texas; in Sindelfingen and Heidelberg in Germany; the full-service Marriott Queensway in Hong Kong; and Marriott Vacation Club timeshare complexes in Desert Springs, California, and Panama City, Florida.

Valerie Knauff

Director of Graphics
Senior Associate

When Valerie Knauff started working at Design Group in 1994, she was a student intern and art major attending the University of Maryland in Baltimore County. At the time, the firm's graphics "division" consisted solely of her and one full-time employee. Its role was little more than to provide very basic graphic support for the firm's architectural projects. From those modest beginnings, graphics has grown into a bona fide, seven-person department that provides everything from elaborate two- and three-dimensional feature graphics to directional signage and promotional brochures for a variety of clients, including an increasing number who seek out Design Group just for graphic design. The transformation is as much attributable to the creative talents of Knauff and her graphic design colleagues as it is to her educational skills—she has invested considerable time and energy into helping the firm's architects understand and respect the important role that graphic design can play in their projects.

Knauff's own educational background in visual art has transferred well to commercial design. (Fittingly, she's an admirer of surrealist Salvador Dali, whose work has been criticized by some as being too commercial.) A versatile designer with special strengths in print and corporate identity, Knauff favors a minimalist approach to graphic design. Logo development, in particular, attracts her because of the freedom it gives to initiate a visual identity. Abstract influences come through in her work, such as in the logos for the Aldhiyafa retail center in Mecca, Saudi Arabia, the Millennia hotel and shopping complex in Ankara, Turkey, and Cape Town's Cavendish Square in South Africa.

Nearly all of Knauff's professional career has been with Design Group. She became director of graphics in 1998, and presides over a department that offers a full range of graphic design services, including corporate identity, environmental graphics, informational and directional graphics, print and promotional materials, and web site design. She is a member of the Society of Environmental Graphic Designers and the International Sign Association.

Pipat Esara

Director of Art
Senior Associate

The type of conceptual design created by Pipat Esara is a sometimes-overlooked aspect of architecture, and only a tiny percentage of all architects use it. Esara's renderings are deceptively simple, translating a concept for a three-dimensional, built environment onto a sheet of paper in ways that not only convey its mass, scale and proportion, but that also bring that environment to life. This is of obvious benefit to a firm which, from the earliest stages of a project, wants a client to "get it." But a good rendering can also help to clarify a project in the minds of others in the firm who are working on it.

Esara came to the United States from his native Thailand in the early 1970s, expecting to continue the kind of work he had been doing there as a project architect. Although he sometimes misses the other aspects of his trade, Esara's uncanny knack for doing renderings is what has defined his career for most of the past twenty-five years. By his own estimation, he has done thousands of renderings, including virtually all of Design Group's since he joined the firm in 1992. He is one of the most prolific practitioners of what may be a fading art form, as more firms turn to computer renderings as an acceptable, cheaper, and easier-to-produce alternative to their hand-drawn counterparts.

Esara has a bachelor degree in architecture from Bangkok's Chulalongkorn University, and a master in urban design from Catholic University in Washington, DC. When he is not drawing buildings, he enjoys painting, photography, and spending time with his family.

■ Indicates projects featured in Selected and Current Works.
Chronological list by year of design.

1999

ICSC Convention Design
Dallas, TX, USA, various

ICSC Exhibit Booth DDG, Inc.,
Las Vegas, NV, USA, various

Aldhiyafa ■
Mecca, Saudi Arabia

Barnes & Noble
Washington, DC, USA

Barnes & Noble
Bridgehampton, NY, USA

Baytown, Destin
FL, USA

Charlottesville Town Center
Charlottesville, VA, USA

Chesapeake Bay Inn
Stevensonville, MD, USA

Chesapeake Resort & Conference Center
Easton, MD, USA

Courtyard by Marriott Emeryville
Emeryville, CA, USA

Dallas Main Street
Dallas, TX, USA

Destin Town Center
Destin, FL, USA

Detroit Entertainment District
Detroit, MI, USA

Fairfax Corner ■
Fairfax, VA, USA

Festival Park Leganes
Madrid, Spain

Festival Park Mallorca ■
Palma de Mallorca, Spain

Gateway, Expo X-plore
Durban, South Africa

Legacy Place ■
Palm Beach Gardens, FL, USA

Lifetime Fitness
Columbus, OH, USA

Marriott Vacation Club International
Legend's Edge
Edge Bay Point, FL, USA

Marriott Vacation Club International Shadow
Ridge
Desert Springs, CA, USA

Merchants Square ■
Williamsburg, VA, USA

Muvico Arundel Mills
Glen Burnie, MD, USA

Muvico BayWalk
St. Petersburg, FL, USA

Muvico City Place
West Palm Beach, FL, USA

Muvico Germantown
Memphis, TN, USA

Paarl Mall
Paarl, South Africa

Paradise Park ■
Davie, FL, USA

Prague Market
Prague, Czech Republic

Rock Springs Town Center
Bethesda, MD, USA

Sheraton Heliopolis
Cairo, Egypt

The Shops at Liberty Place Retail
Philadelphia, PA, USA

Unicentro El Marques ■
Caracas, Venezuela

Vanderbilt Galleria
Bonita Springs, FL, USA

Wisconsin Avenue Marketplace
Washington, DC, USA

1998

Brandenburg Park
Berlin, Germany

Cascades, Durban
South Africa

Central Park Town Center
Atlanta, GA, USA

Chelsea Market
Pittsburgh, PA, USA

Colonial Plaza ■
Caracas, Venezuela

Courtyard by Marriott Chicago Downtown
Chicago, IL, USA

Courtyard by Marriott San Francisco
San Francisco, CA, USA

Courtyard by Marriott Tysons Corner
McClean, VA, USA

Easton Town Center Fashion District
Columbus, OH, USA

Mariner's Cove ■
Gocek, Turkey

Hartford Civic Center
Hartford, CT, USA

Holiday Inn Tysons Corner
McClean, VA, USA

Marriott Appleton Inn
Tinton Falls, USA

Marriott New York
New York, NY, USA

Marriott Tinton Falls
Marina del Rey, CA, USA

Millennia Tower
Ankara, Turkey

Muvico Birkdale Village
Charlotte, NC, USA

Muvico Centro Ybor
Tampa, FL, USA

Muvico Concordville
Concordville, PA, USA

Muvico Gainesville
Gainesville, FL, USA

Muvico Hialeah
Hialeah, FL, USA

Muvico Jacksonville
Jacksonville, FL, USA

Muvico Peabody Place
Memphis, TN, USA

Muvico Tampa Palms ■
Tampa Palms, FL, USA

Pointe Orlando Graphics ■
Orlando, FL, USA

Ramada Hotel Sindelfingen
Sindelfingen, Germany

Muvico Paradise 24 Davie, Florida, USA

Expo X-plore Durban, South Africa

Colonial Plaza Caracas, Venezuela

e Zone@Rosebank Johannesburg, South Africa

2000

Graphic Design: USA
American Graphic Design Award
Corporate holiday greeting card for
Development Design Group, Inc.
Baltimore, Maryland, USA

Signs of the Times
First Place Design Awards
Muvico Paradise 24
Davie, Florida, USA

Signs of the Times
Honorable Mention
Muvico "Drive-In"
Pompano Beach, Florida, USA

ICSC Design & Development Award
*Design Award—Innovative Design &
Construction of a New Project*
Easton Town Center
Columbus, Ohio, USA

ICSC Design & Development Award
*Certificate of Merit—Innovative Design &
Construction of a New Project*
Tai Mall
Taipei, Taiwan

ICSC Design & Development Award
*Certificate of Merit—Renovation or
Expansion of an Existing Project*
Montrose Crossing
Rockville, Maryland, USA

1999

Scheufelen North America, Inc.
Award of Excellence
Corporate origami Christmas card design
for Development Design Group, Inc.
Baltimore, Maryland, USA

Society of Environmental Graphic Design
Juror's Award
Muvico Paradise 24
Davie, Florida, USA

ISP/VM+SD International Store Design
Competition
*First Place Design Award—Entertainment
Facility*
Muvico Paradise 24
Davie, Florida, USA

ICSC Design & Development Award
*Certificate of Merit—Renovation/Expansion
of an Existing Project*
Cavendish Square
Johannesburg, South Africa

1998

FIABCI Prix d'Excellence
Category Winner—Retail Properties
Eastgate
Harare, Zimbabwe

ICSC Design & Development Award
*Certificate of Merit—Renovation/Expansion
of an Existing Project*
The Streets of Mayfair
Miami, Florida, USA

ICSC Design & Development Award
*Design Award—Innovative Design of a New
Project*
Westgate
Harare, Zimbabwe

DuPont Benedictus Award
*Certificate of Recognition—Innovation in
Arch. Laminated Glass*
Akmerkez Etiler
Istanbul, Turkey

DuPont Benedictus Award
*Certificate of Recognition—Innovation in
Arch. Laminated Glass*
Cavendish Square
Cape Town, South Africa

DuPont Benedictus Award
*Certificate of Recognition—Innovation in
Arch. Laminated Glass*
Eastgate
Harare, Zimbabwe

DuPont Benedictus Award
*Certificate of Recognition—Innovation in
Arch. Laminated Glass*
Mal Puri Indah
Jakarta, Indonesia

1997

FIABCI Prix d'Excellence
Finalist—Retail Properties
Akmerkez Etiler
Istanbul, Turkey

FIABCI Prix d'Excellence
Finalist—Retail Properties
CocoWalk
Miami, Florida, USA

FIABCI Prix d'Excellence
Finalist—Retail Properties
Old Orchard
Chicago, Illinois, USA

ICSC Design & Development Award
*Certificate of Merit—Innovative Design of a
New Project*
Eastgate
Harare, Zimbabwe

Ramada Renaissance Heidelberg Hotel
Heidelberg, Germany

The Zone@Rosebank ■
Johannesburg, South Africa

Vista Real
Quito, Ecuador

1997

BayWalk
St. Petersburg, FL, USA

Carlton Center
Johannesburg, South Africa

Cempaka Metropolitan
Jakarta, Indonesia

Cocowalk, Bogota
Bogota, Colombia

Cornell Towne Centre ■
Toronto, Ontario, Canada

Deer Park
Chicago, IL, USA

Dreamland Shopping Resort ■
Cairo, Egypt

Easton Esplanade
Columbus, OH, USA

Fountain Square
Nashville, TN, USA

Gading Serpong
Tangerang, Indonesia

Gunung Sahari
Jakarta, Indonesia

Hagarmenah Regency
Bandung, Indonesia

Lenox Marketplace
Atlanta, GA, USA

Menara Jakarta
Jakarta, Indonesia

Muvico Boca Raton
Boca Raton, FL, USA

Muvico Paradise 24 ■
Davie, FL, USA

Muvico Drive-In ■
Pompano Beach, FL, USA

Palmera ■
Cairo, Egypt

Parque Brickell
Jakarta, Indonesia

Ramada Renaissance Sanur
Bali, Indonesia

Scottsdale Waterfront
Scottsdale, AZ, USA

Senopati ■
Jakarta, Indonesia

Taba Golden Coast ■
Taba, Egypt

TaiMall ■
Taipei, Taiwan

Urbana Town Center
Urbana, MD, USA

Virginia Beach Town Center
Virginia Beach, VA, USA

1996

Alam Namoriam
Medan, Sumatra, Indonesia

Alandha Sentul
Bogor, Indonesia

AMI Japan
Moriya, Japan

Bali Sanur Hotel
Bali, Indonesia

Bali Sanur Sanur Plaza
Bali, Indonesia

BNI City Super Block
Jakarta, Indonesia

Cavendish Square ■
Cape Town, South Africa

Centro Ybor
Tampa, FL, USA

Charleston Shopping Center
Charleston, SC, USA

Country Club Plaza
Kansas City, MO, USA

Danau Bogor Raya Marketing Brochure
Bogor, Indonesia

Dreamland Master Plan ■
Cairo, Egypt

Grand Bromo Resort
East Java, Indonesia

Howard Street Redevelopment Plan
Baltimore, MD, USA

Johannesburg Revitalization Master Plan ■
Johannesburg, South Africa

Kansas City Power & Light
Kansas City, MO, USA

Kentlands Market Square ■
Gaithersburg, MD, USA

Marriott New Orleans
New Orleans, LA, USA

Marriott Zurich
Zurich, Switzerland

Menlyn Park ■
Pretoria, South Africa

MovieWalk
Babelsberg/Potsdam, Germany

Newport on the Levee ■
Newport, KY, USA

Plaza San Marino
Guayaquil, Ecuador

Private Country Residence ■
Baltimore, MD, USA

USArts District ■
Washington, DC, USA

Zonk'izizwe ■
Midrand, South Africa

1995

American Dream
Silver Spring, MD, USA

Bali Benoa Marina
Bali, Indonesia

Bali Isola Resort
Tabanan, Bali, Indonesia

Batam Laguna Villas
Batam Island, Indonesia

Citicorp Center Retail
New York, NY, USA

Danau Bogor Raya
Bogor, Indonesia

Dubai Blue Coast ■
Dubai, United Arab Emirates

Easton Town Center ■
Columbus, OH, USA

Cempaka Metropolitan Jakarta, Indonesia

Dreamland Shopping Resort Cairo, Epypt

Cavendish Square Cape Town, South Africa

Dubai Blue Coast Dubai, UAE

ICSC Design & Development Award
Design Award—Renovation/Expansion of
an Existing Project
Old Orchard
Chicago, Illinois, USA

1996

ICSC Design & Development Award
Design Award—Innovative Design of a New
Project
Akmerkez Etiler
Istanbul, Turkey

ICSC Design & Development Award
Certificate of Merit—Innovative Design of a
New Project
The Marketplace at Cascades Town Center
Loudoun County, Virginia, USA

1995

ICSC–Europe Design & Development Award
First Place Design Award—Best New
Shopping Center in Europe
Akmerkez Etiler
Istanbul, Turkey

Pacific Coast Builders Conference
Gold Nugget Award
Grand Award—Best Land Plan
Legend City/Kota Legenda
Bekasi, Indonesia

1994

FIABCI Prix d'Excellence
Special Mention Award—Leisure Properties
Taman Impian Jaya Ancol
North Jakarta, Indonesia

*Pacific Coast Builders Conference
Gold Nugget Award Merit Award—Best
Commercial Retail
Citraland Centre Grogol
Jakarta, Indonesia

Pacific Coast Builders Conference
Gold Nugget Award
Merit Award—Best New Town Plan
Taruma Resort
Bogor, Indonesia

1993

*ICSC Design & Development Award
Certificate of Merit—Innovative Design of a
New Project
Pondok Indah Mall
Jakarta, Indonesia

Pacific Coast Builders Conference
Gold Nugget Award
Merit Award—Best Commercial Project,
Regional/Power Retail
Pondok Indah Mall
Jakarta, Indonesia

*Pacific Coast Builders Conference
Gold Nugget Award
Merit Award—Best New Town Plan
Taman Impian Jaya Ancol
North Jakarta, Indonesia

*Associated Builders and Contractors, Inc.
Outstanding Project Award
Perring Plaza
Baltimore, Maryland, USA

*1992

ICSC Design & Development Award
First Place Award—Innovative Design of a
New Project
CocoWalk
Miami, Florida, USA

Pacific Coast Builders Conference
Gold Nugget Award
Grand Award—Best New Town Plan
Pantai Indah Kapuk
Jakarta, Indonesia

Pacific Coast Builders Conference
Gold Nugget Award
Site Plan of the Year & Best of Show
Pantai Indah Kapuk
Jakarta, Indonesia

ULI Award of Excellence
Award—Small-Scale Commercial/Retail
Development
CocoWalk
Miami, Florida, USA

Pacific Coast Builders Conference
Gold Nugget Award
Merit Award—Best Commercial Retail
Project
Scottsdale Galleria
Scottsdale, Arizona, USA

*1991

National Mall Monitor Centers of Excellence
Honorable Mention
CocoWalk
Miami, Florida, USA

City of Miami
Beautification and Environment Award
CocoWalk
Miami, Florida, USA

Galeria Glodok Signage & Graphics
Jakarta, Indonesia

Graha Haripan
West Surabaya, Indonesia

Holiday Inn Semarang
Semarang, Indonesia

Holiday Inn Yogyakarta
Yogyakarta, Indonesia

Jatinegara Plaza Signage
Jakarta, Indonesia

Kaneh High Technology Park
Drom HaSharon, Israel

Kebon Melati ■
Jakarta, Indonesia

Kemer Country ■
Istanbul, Turkey

Kota Kasablanka Anggana Radisson
Jakarta, Indonesia

Kozyatagi
Istanbul, Turkey

Marriott Bali
Bali, Indonesia

Marriott Galeria Glodok ■
Jakarta, Indonesia

Marriott Sentral Solo
Solo, Indonesia

Marriott Surabaya
Surabaya, Indonesia

Marriott Way Halim
Lampung City, Sumatra, Indonesia

Pakuwon Golf Estates
Surabaya, Indonesia

Pantai Kapuknaga ■
West Java, Indonesia

Pondok Indah Galleria & Hotel
Jakarta, Indonesia

Robertson Walk ■
Singapore

Sheraton International Hotel @ BWI
Baltimore, MD, USA

Telaga Kahuripan ■
Parung, Indonesia

Tunjungan Plaza IV
Surabaya, Indonesia

Way Halim Graphics & Signage
Lampung City, Sumatra, Indonesia

World Trade Center
New York, NY, USA

1994

Bay Landing Master Plan
Naples, FL, USA

Bogor Mountain Terraces
Bogor, Indonesia

Bogor Panorama Permai
Bogor, Indonesia

Cempaka Mas
Jakarta, Indonesia

Dharmala Aldiron Building ■
Jakarta, Indonesia

Dharmala Imeco
Jakarta, Indonesia

East Bekasi Shopping Center
East Bekasi, Indonesia

Gandaria
Jakarta, Indonesia

The Grove
Houston, TX, USA

Key West Outlet Center
Key West, FL, USA

Le Meridien Hotel
Jakarta, Indonesia

Kota Legenda ■
Bekasi, Indonesia

Marbella Residencia ■
Anyer, Indonesia

Market at 30th Street Station
Philadelphia, PA, USA

Market at 30th Street Station Graphics
Philadelphia, PA, USA

Montrose Crossing ■
Rockville, MD, USA

Pantai Hijau Master Plan
Jakarta, Indonesia

Park Royal Hotel & Service Apartments ■
Jakarta, Indonesia

Sheraton International Hotel
Virginia Beach, VA, USA

Taman Tubagus Raya
Jakarta, Indonesia

1993

Bandung SuperMal
Bandung, Indonesia

Beachside Aruba ■
Palm Beach, Aruba, Dutch Caribbean

Easton Club
Easton, MD, USA

Hanoi Plaza Hotel
Hanoi, Vietnam

McDonogh Crossroads
Baltimore, MD, USA

Puri Indah Master Plan
West Jakarta, Indonesia

Streets of Mayfair ■
Coconut Grove, FL, USA

Taman Besar Ijen
Malang, Indonesia

Taruma Resort ■
Bogor, Indonesia

*1992

Aksel Masterplan
Istanbul, Turkey

Bintaro Jaya Garden City Master Plan
Jakarta, Indonesia

Eastgate ■
Harare, Zimbabwe

Festival Shopping Center
Honolulu, HI, USA

Galeria Glodok
Jakarta, Indonesia

Harbour Island Beach Resort
Harbour Island, Bahamas

Marketplace at Cascades Town Center ■
Sterling, VA, USA

Easton Town Center Columbus, Ohio, USA

Kota Legenda Bekasi, Indonesia

Beachside Aruba Aruba, Dutch Caribbean

Yuan Hong City Fuzhou, China

National Mall Monitor Centers of Excellence
Honorable Mention
The Factory Shops at San Marcos
San Marcos, Texas, USA

*1990

American Society of Association Executives
(ASAE)
Diamond Award
1990 ICSC Convention Leasing Mall
Las Vegas, Nevada, USA

ICSC Design & Development Award
*Certificate of Merit—Renovation/Expansion
of an Existing Project*
Northwest Plaza
St. Louis, Missouri, USA

NAIOP, Maryland & DC Chapters
Design Award of Excellence
McDonogh Crossroads
Baltimore, Maryland, USA

NAIOP Maryland/DC Chapter
Design Award of Excellence
SurgiCenter at McDonogh Crossroads
Baltimore, Maryland, USA

*1989

ARIDO Design Award
Silver—Adaptive Re-Use
Galleria at Southpointe
Pittsburgh, Pennsylvania, USA

Buildings Modernization Design Award
Honorable Mention
Miller Hill Mall
Duluth, Minnesota, USA

Buildings Modernization Design Award
Honorable Mention
Towne East Square
Wichita, Kansas, USA

ICSC Design & Development Award
*First Place Award—Excellence in
Renovation Design*
Burlington Mall
Boston, Massachusetts, USA

ICSC Design & Development Award
*Certificate of Merit—Innovative Design of a
New Project*
Fifth Avenue Place
Pittsburgh, Pennsylvania, USA

ICSC Design & Development Award
*Certificate of Merit - Excellence in
Renovation Design*
Towne East Square
Wichita, Kansas, USA

Signs of the Times Design Award
*First Place Environmental Graphics &
Signage*
Moorestown Mall
Moorestown, New Jersey, USA

Hampton Civic Association
*Design Award for Excellence in Civic
Improvements*
Newmarket South
Newport News, Virginia, USA

*1988

ARIDO Design Award
Silver—Shopping Center Design
Fountain Square
Nashville, Tennessee, USA

ICSC Design & Development Award
*First Place Award—Innovative Design of a
New Project*
Fountain Square
Nashville, Tennessee, USA

NAIOP, Maryland & DC Chapters
*Design Award of Excellence—Mixed-Use
Suburban Office Buildings*
McDonogh Crossroads
Baltimore, Maryland, USA

*1987

ARIDO Design Award
Bronze—Shopping Center Design
Moorestown Mall
Moorestown, New Jersey, USA

ARIDO Design Award
Silver—Shopping Center Design
Belvedere Square
Baltimore, Maryland, USA

ICSC Design & Development Award
First Place—Design Award of Excellence
Belvedere Square
Baltimore, Maryland, USA

National Mall Monitor Centers of Excellence
First Place Design Award
Belvedere Square
Baltimore, Maryland, USA

National Mall Monitor Centers of Excellence
First Place Design Award
Galtier Plaza
St. Paul, Minnesota, USA

National Mall Monitor Centers of Excellence
Honorable Mention
The Mall at Mill Creek
Baltimore, Maryland, USA

Pasadena Gardens
Jakarta, Indonesia

Plaza Yogya Hotel ■
Yogyakarta, Java, Indonesia

Private Penthouse Residence ■
Istanbul, Turkey

Radisson Plaza Suite Hotel ■
Surabaya, Indonesia

Taman Impian Jaya Ancol
Jakarta, Indonesia

World Trade Center
Baltimore, MD, USA

Yuan Hong City ■
Fuzhou, PRC

*1991

Akmerkez Etiler Shopping Center ■
Istanbul, Turkey

Bali Kuta Galleria
Bali, Indonesia

Baltimore International Yachting Center ■
Baltimore, MD, USA

Bur Juman Centre ■
Dubai, United Arab Emirates

BWI Airport Hotel
Baltimore, MD, USA

Golf View Terraces ■
Jakarta, Indonesia

Green Valley Town Center
Las Vegas, NV, USA

Holiday Inn Bali Hai Resort ■
Bali, Indonesia

Kentlands Square Shopping Center ■
Gaithersburg, MD, USA

Pondok Indah Golf Clubhouse
Jakarta, Indonesia

*1990

Burlington Mall
Burlington, MA, USA

Democracy Plaza
Bethesda, MD, USA

Dubai Office Building
Dubai, United Arab Emirates

Pantai Indah Kapuk Master Plan
Jakarta, Indonesia

Vizcaya at Dune Allen ■
Walton County, FL, USA

Westgate ■
Harare, Zimbabwe

*1989

Citraland Centre Grogol ■
Jakarta, Indonesia

Fifth Avenue Place
Pittsburgh, PA, USA

Kapuk Golf Clubhouse ■
Jakarta, Indonesia

Lynnhaven Mall Renovation and Expansion
Virginia Beach, VA, USA

Pondok Indah Mall
Jakarta, Indonesia

The Courtyard
Destin, FL, USA

*1988

Al Ghurair Center
Dubai, United Arab Emirates

Al Souk al Markhazi
Dubai, United Arab Emirates

Edinburgh Maritime
Edinburgh, Scotland

Northwest Plaza
St Louis, MO, USA

Old Orchard ■
Chicago, IL, USA

San Marcos Factory Shops
San Marcos, TX, USA

Warehouse Row ■
Chattanooga, TN, USA

*1987

Al Manal Centre
Dubai, United Arab Emirates

Burnsville Center
Burnsville, MN, USA

Cocowalk ■
Miami, FL, USA

Galleria at Southpointe
Pittsburgh, PA, USA

Harbourside
Harbourside, NJ, USA

Galtier Plaza
St. Paul, MN USA

Maplewood Mall
Maplewood, MN, USA

Reading Station
Reading, PA, USA

Scottsdale Galleria
Scottsdale, AZ, USA

*1986–1979

Belvedere Square
Baltimore, MD, USA

Claypool Court
Indianapolis, IN, USA

Galtier Plaza
St Paul, MN, USA

Golden Ring Mall
Baltimore, MD, USA

Maplewood Mall
Minneapolis, MN, USA

Miller Hill Mall
Duluth, MN, USA

Moorstown Mall
Moorstown, NJ, USA

North Riverside Park
Chicago, IL, USA

Rainbow Center
Niagara Falls, NY, USA

Riverplace
Minneapolis, MN, USA

Springfield Park
Springfield, IL, USA

Towne East Mall
Wichita, KS, USA

Akmerkez Etiler Istanbul, Turkey

1991

Vizcaya at Dune Allen Destin, Florida, USA

1990

Old Orchard Chicago, Illinois

1988

Cocowalk Miami, Florida

1987

ICSC Design & Development Award
First Place - Design Award of Excellence
Galtier Plaza
St. Paul, Minnesota, USA

*1986

ICSC Design & Development Award
First Place—Design Award of Excellence
Claypool Court
Indianapolis, Indiana, USA

Signs of the Times Design Award
*Award of Excellence—Environmental
Graphics & Print Casebooks*
Riverplace
Minneapolis, Minnesota, USA

Signs of the Times Design Award
First Place—Electric Sign Graphic
Galtier Plaza
St. Paul, Minnesota, USA

*1985

ARIDO Design Award
Gold—Adaptive Re-Use
Riverplace
Minneapolis, Minnesota, USA

ICSC Design & Development Award
First Place—Design Award of Excellence
Riverplace
Minneapolis, Minnesota, USA

Maryland Society of the AIA
Design Award of Excellence
Riverplace
Minneapolis, Minnesota, USA

Metro. Indianapolis Development Comm.
Design Award of Excellence
Claypool Court
Indianapolis, Indiana, USA

Metro. Indianapolis Development Comm.
*Monumental Design Award for
Outstanding Development Project*
Claypool Court
Indianapolis, Indiana, USA

National Mall Monitor Centers of Excellence
First Place Design Award
Claypool Court
Indianapolis, Indiana, USA

Maryland Society of the AIA
Honor Award for Excellence
Fork Union Military Academy
Fork Union, Virginia, USA

Committee for Downtown Indianapolis
Honors Award
*Outstanding Contribution to the
Beautification of Downtown*
Claypool Court
Indianapolis, Indiana, USA

*1984

AIA – Baltimore Chapter
First Place Award for Design Excellence
Riverplace
Minneapolis, Minnesota, USA

CUE Design Award
Project of Design Excellence
Riverplace
Minneapolis, Minnesota, USA

NESA Signage Award
First Place
Riverplace
Minneapolis, Minnesota, USA

ULI Award of Excellence
Award—Small-Scale Development
Rainbow Center
Niagara Falls, New York, USA

*1983

ICSC Design & Development Award
First Place—Design Award of Excellence
Springfield Park
Springfield, Pennsylvania, USA

Baltimore Chapter AIA
First Place Award for Design Excellence
Rainbow Center
Niagara Falls, New York, USA

Maryland Chapter ASID
First Place Design Award
Westminster Hall
Baltimore, Maryland, USA

Baltimore Chapter AIA
First Place Award for Design Excellence
Glen Oaks Farm
Baltimore, Maryland, USA

*1982

ICSC Design & Development Award
First Place—Design Award of Excellence
Rainbow Center
Niagara Falls, New York, USA

* Under the names of our former firms:
D.I. Architecture, Inc. or D.I. Design &
Development Consultants, Inc.

Bibliography

Aguilar, L. "Maryland: The year in review: Major mall proposed for Silver Spring," The Washington Post (28 December 1995), p. M01.

Ahlers, M. "Lorenz building plans called crowning glory," Montgomery Business Journal (1984).

Anders, C.M. "Building on international success: Reporter's notebook from PCBC," San Francisco Examiner (2 July 1995), p. E1.

Andreone, J. DCA Theater Design Charette (February 1998).

Atkinson, J. "Emulating the termite, a new approach to architectural design," The Zimbabwean Review (October 1995), pp. 16–19.

Beasley, K. "Theater design gets national focus," Paraplegia News (1 April 1998), p. 68.

Benson, B. "Galleria construction ends, leasing in high gear," The Pittsburgh Business Times (vol. 8, no. 23, 23-29 January 1989).

Berlin, H. "Old Orchard harvests fruits of its labor," Shopping Center World (vol. 28, no. 5, 1 May 1999), pp. 216–17.

Bivins, R. "Home of tomorrow—predictions for the housing industry include low-cost, one-room mod-pod," Houston Chronicle (30 January 1995), p. 1.

Blank, E. "Galleria getting 6-screen movie complex," The Pittsburgh Press (1 February 1989).

Carney, K. "International marketing workshop," World Trade Center, Baltimore, Maryland (22 February 1996).

Chang, J.Y. "Global trends in serviced apartment design and development," Presented to Serviced Apartments Conference in Taipei, Taiwan. (28–29 October 1997).

Clark, J.B. "Leasing, tenant mix & placemaking: Avoiding cookie-cutter pitfalls," Presented at ECI Entertainment Retail Conference in Los Angeles, CA. (22 January 1999).

Clemence, S. "Americans abroad: How baltimore-based Development Design Group is changing the world," The Daily Record—Buildout (March 2000), p. 5.

Como, D. "Triple Five redesigns American Dream," Real Estate Journal Interactive (24 November 1995).

Crawford, J. "A grand opening at the Galleria, marble, mime, ballet greet patrons," Pittsburgh Post Gazette (4 March 1989).

Davis, R. "St. Petersburg's BayWalk to be Mediterranean plaza," St. Petersburg Times (15 July 1998), p. 5.

Davis, R. "BayWalk will be a Mediterranean plaza," St. Petersburg Times (12 July 1998), p. 3.

DeSimone, E. "Center profile: The debut of a small town," Shopping Center World (vol. 28, no. 12, 1 November 1999).

Development Design Group, Inc. "Awards given to Maryland's international leaders," World View (March 1997).

Development Design Group, Inc. "Cavendish Square," Architect & Builder, South Africa (September 1998).

Development Design Group, Inc. "New shopping center," Planning Magazine, South Africa (vol. 65, no. 7, July 1999).

Development Design Group, Inc. "Old Mutual Partnership wins international award," SAPOA News Update (April 1997).

Development Design Group, Inc. "Resort development Dreamland," MIPIM News (February 1999).

Development Design Group, Inc. Akmerkez Shop Vision Magazine (February 1998).

Development Design Group, Inc. "Baltimore design firm to pare down mega mall," Real Estate Journal Interactive (3 November 1995).

Development Design Group, Inc. "Eastgate: Matter of fact," The Financial Gazette, Harare, Zimbabwe (15 April 1999).

Donoghue, E.O. "Bonita shopping center planned," News-Press, Fort Myers, Florida (10 June 1994), p. 13.

Dorsey, B. "The new town square," Signs of the Times (vol. 207, no. 2, 1985).

Dunlop, B. "Charette promises renewal for Miami's Decorator's Row," Architectural Record (January 1998), p. 31.

Engen, J.R. "How exports rescued my company," World Trade (vol. 8, no. 6, July 1995), p. 22.

Federal Document Clearing House. "Trip of the Vice President and Deputy President Mbeki to Baltimore," Government Press Releases (22 July 1996).

Fickes, M. "Can Columbus discover a new downtown?" Shopping Center World (vol. 27, no. 5, 30 May 1998).

Forgey, B. "A different dream for Silver Spring," The Washington Post (11 November 1995), p. C01.

Gallagher, J. "Upscale retail in the suburbs," Pittsburgh Post Gazette (1989).

Gluck, A. "Local ties to South Africa encouraged: Business partnerships are key, leaders say," The Baltimore Sun (23 July 1996), p. 1C.

Gogoll, T. "Rich history: Tampa center banks on past to draw future crowds," Shopping Centers Today (1 August 1999).

Gunts, E. "Millennium sculpture a success, wishes: Thousands have visited the structure built downtown," The Baltimore Sun (6 January 2000).

Gunts, E. "City's monument to the millennium, sculpture: Residents and visitors will be allowed to express their thoughts and dreams for the future on the city's planned 'Millennium Message,'" The Baltimore Sun (18 October 1999), p. 1E.

Gunts, E. "Bromo hits the beach: The city's landmark tower will lend its good looks to a tropical shopping and recreation center," The Baltimore Sun (8 August 1999), p. 2F.

Hance, M. "Tennessee is slowing, but still going," Shopping Center World (June 1990), pp. 71–73.

Hancock, J. "Rioting in Indonesia sends chill through local firms," The Baltimore Sun (16 May 1998), p. 1A.

Hancock, J. "Economic woes in Asia generate worries in U.S. Damage to companies, job losses predicted, but extent is elusive; Upside is low-cost goods," The Baltimore Sun (8 February 1998), p. 1A.

Hancock, J. "Maryland companies need to climb the export learning curve," The Baltimore Sun (15 April 1996), p. 9C.

Hansell, M. "Notice—Animal Architecture," Engineering News Record (vol. 222, no. 7, 21 February 2000), p. 115.

Hassell, G. "Food, shopping and fun—The Grove complex finds a home in Stafford," Houston Chronicle (17 January 1995), p. 1.

Haynes, J.P. "Cocowalk can have a positive influence in Grove," The Coconut Grover (vol. 2, no. 8, August 1990), p. 2.

Higgs, R. "Shoppertainment," Presented to SAPOA in Cape Town and Johannesburg, Republic of South Africa (26–28 October 1999).

Higgs, R. "Global real estate forum: The vision of global real estate in the future," Presented to FIABCI-USA International Real Estate Federation, US Chapter in Washington, DC (25 March 1999).

Higgs, R. "An African experience: A conference and tour of shopping centers in South Africa," Presented in Sun City, Republic of South Africa (5 September 1998).

Higgs, R. "Shopping 2000: The shape of shopping to come," Presented at Singapore Retailer's Association Conference in Singapore (9–10 July 1998).

Higgs, R. "Asia on sale: A look at global trends or a real world view from someone in the service sector," Presented at FIABCI International Real Estate Federation Spring Annual Meeting in Washington, DC (28 March 1998).

Higgs, R. "Doing business in South Africa," Presented at the World Trade Center Institute in Baltimore, MD. (27 January 1998).

Higgs, R. "Southeast Asia: Managing risk," Presented to World Trade Center Institute in Baltimore, MD (3 December 1997).

Higgs, R. and Dixon, S. "Harare inner city partnership conference," Presented to National Property Association in Harare, Zimbabwe (12–14 November 1997).

Higgs, R. "The shopping center as art: Global trends in mixed-use and shopping center development," Presented at Taiwan City Development Conference in Taipei, Taiwan (25 September 1997).

Higgs, R. "Plan globally, design locally," Presented at Global Super Projects Conference in Paris, France (9 June 1997).

Higgs, R. "Architecture as business," Presented at Loyola College of Maryland in Baltimore, MD (22 March 1997).

Higgs, R. "The internationalization of real estate development and the impact of technology on modern development both domestically and abroad," Presented at FIABCI-USA Global Real Estate Forum in Washington, DC (20 March 1997).

Higgs, R. "International marketplace," Presented to The Johns Hopkins University MA in International Real Estate Class in Baltimore, MD (21 January 1997).

Higgs, R. "Architecture is architecture and business is business and never the twain shall meet: Generating global design business when your company is not world-famous," Presented to Department of Architecture at Howard University in Washington, DC (1997).

Higgs, R. "Building your business in Indonesia: Construction and related services," Presented at World Trade Center in Baltimore, Maryland (11 April 1996).

Higgs, R. "What's hiding behind the hype: A look at real global retail trends," Presented to SAPOA in Cape Town, Republic of South Africa (21 February 1996).

Higgs, R. "How effective design and planning improves shopping center profitability," Presented at the 2nd Annual Middle East Conference on Shopping Centres in Dubai, UAE (20–21 November 1995).

Higgs, R. "Planning and designing your super center," Presented at the 1995 Asia Pacific Super Centers Conference in Singapore (25°27 April 1995).

Higgs, R. "International design and its effect on US retailing and shopping centers," Presented at CRAMMM Conference in Daytona Beach, FL (7 February 1994).

Higgs, R. "Construction services consulting in China: Experience with mixed-use projects," Presented at World Trade Center Institute Conference — Trading with China, China Anhui Delegation in Baltimore, MD (10 November 1993).

Higgs, R. "Doing business in Indonesia," Presented at International Day in Washington, DC (14 May 1993).

Higgs, R. "Global retail development and merchandising trends observed," Presented to British Florida Chamber of Commerce in Coral Gables, FL (20 November 1992).

Higgs, R. "Global design trends in the African marketplace," Presented at 1st African Congress of Shopping Centers in Sun City, Republic of South Africa (23–15 August 1992).

Higgs, R. "Business opportunities in Southeast Asia: Generating service industry business in Singapore when your company is not world-famous," Presented at the World Trade Center Institute in Baltimore, MD (16 July 1992).

Jaipul, L. "Retail center on its way to Glen Oaks," New York Daily News (3 August 1988).

Kaiser, R. "Persistence pays off for award winners," Baltimore Business Journal (vol. 14, no. 40, 17 February 1997), p. 12.

Kamin, B. "Shopping for an identity, renovated Old Orchard," Chicago Tribune (17 September 1995), p. 16.

Kamin, B. "The Wright Way Fall brings a bonanza of exhibits focusing on the Prairie School," Chicago Tribune (7 September 1995), p. 10A.

Keenan, T. "Money-spinning mall rolls tenants along," Finance Week, Johannesburg, South Africa (vol. 76, no. 21, 28 May–3 June 1998), p. 28.

King, C. "Retail News," National Real Estate Investor (vol.38, no. 6, June 1996), p. 14.

Levine, F. "Sexy assets grab Hollywood's attention," Variety (10–16 June 1996), pp. 9,14.

Locke, D.E. "Fostering Balance," Landscape Online @ www.landscapeonline.com/ lolpages/-editorial/-%20News Departments/BusinessNews/Financia/ 9812FosteringBalance.htm (December 1998).

Lynch, M. "Development Design Group spreads work near and far," The Daily Record, Baltimore, MD (24 May 1993), p. 9.

Lynch, M. "Playing the international card: Development Design Group, Inc.'s timely decision to expand overseas saved firm from a recession that idled 40 percent of Maryland Architects," Warfield's Business Record (21 May 1993), p. 1.

Lynch, M. "Local D.I. Design heads pull buyout," The Daily Record, Baltimore, MD (29 October 1992), p. 3.

Major, M.J. "Asia is next beneficiary of Yankee ingenuity," Shopping Center World (1 May 1994), p. 180.

Marlowe, G. "Export deals keep shipyard shipshape," Richmond Times Dispatch (16 March 1996), p. C1.

McQuaid, K.L. "Architects decide to remain downtown," The Baltimore Sun (3 November 1995), p. 1C.

Paul, D. "Retail and entertainment design firm shopping global markets for business," The Daily Record, Baltimore, MD (4 April 1997), p. 15A.

Radebe, S. "Face-lift surgery brings award for Cavendish Square," Business Day, South Africa (3 June 1999).

Radebe, S. "Drive-in at revamped Menlyn," Business Day, South Africa (11 June 1999), p. 22.

Rimmer, P.J. and Dick, H.W. "Beyond the third world city: The new urban geography in South-east Asia," Urban Studies (vol. 35, no. 12, 1 December 1998).

Samuel, P.D. "From China to Turkey, local architects going global: Is it a Baltimore thing? Local firms like the security that comes from diverse clientele, but face challenges with foreign traditions," The Daily Record, Baltimore, MD (17 September 1998), p. 1D.

Satterfield, D. "CocoWalk's appeal silences the skeptics," The Miami Herald (10 June 1991), p. 7.

Shear, M.D. "A new lease on life? Ambitious renovation aims to resurrect mall's glory days," The Washington Post (24 March 1994).

Shearin, R. "Steiner's talk of the town," Shopping Center Business (August 1999), pp. 52–55.

Simmonds, N. "Correspondent's file: With the economies of Southeast Asia reeling, architects working in the region are facing a difficult future," Architectural Record (April 1998), pp. 47–48.

Slessor, C. "Critical mass — using principles of natural heating, cooling and ventilation," The Architectural Review (September 1996), pp. 36–40.

Smith, M. "A festival for charity - Preview of Galleria in Mount Lebanon to help the Carnegie Hospice," The Pittsburgh Press (2 February 1989).

Smith, M. "Developer's goals lofty for Galleria's shops," The Pittsburgh Press (15 September 1988)

Staff. "1999 superior achievement in design and imaging: Renovated entertainment themed centers," Shopping Center World (vol. 28, no. 5, 1 May 1999).

Staff. "A measure of prosperity," Pittsburgh Post Gazette (11 March 1989).

Staff. "Architecture firm buys itself from foreigners," The Baltimore Sun (24 November 1992), p. 10D.

Staff. "Best in the west, southland home builders, architects dominate Pacific Coast Builders," Los Angeles Times (20 June 1993), p. 10.

Staff. "Bigger boxes, lower rents: Citicorp Center aims for larger chains," Chain Store Age Executive with Shopping Center Age (vol. 71, no. 10, October 1995), p. 128.

Staff. "California builders dominate Gold Nugget competition," Los Angeles Times (25 June 1995).

Staff. "Coconut Grove, Florida to house CocoWalk," Dealmakers Weekly (10 April 1989), p. 6.

Staff. "Constructa US Inc. developing CocoWalk," Southeast Real Estate News (June 1989), p. 8.

Staff. "Educator, dredge maker and architectural firm win Maryland trade awards," The Daily Record, Baltimore, MD (14 February 1997), p. 5A.

Staff. "Four Marylanders were honored by Baltimore's World Trade Center Institute yesterday for achievements in international commerce," The Baltimore Sun Business Digest (14 February 1997), p. 2C.

Staff. "Gold Nugget award winners," San Francisco Examiner (25 June 1995), p. E4.

Staff. "International architecture firm tracks project profitability with customizable accounting software," Design Cost Data (vol. 43, no. 3, 1 May 1998), p. 7.

Staff. "International award for Westgate," The Financial Gazette, Harare, Zimbabwe (21 May 1998).

Staff. "New foreign investment (PMA), projects granted final approvals," Indonesian Investment Highlights (1 May 1995).

Staff. "News In brief: Towson Business Association," The Baltimore Sun (30 May 1994).

Staff. "On the move," The Baltimore Sun (15 February 1993).

Staff. "On the move," The Baltimore Sun (3 January 1994).

Staff. "Pacific Rim country reports architects' search for identity in the face of rapid change," Architectural Record (1 July 1995), p. 37.

Staff. "PMDN and PMA projects approved in third and fourth week of April, 1995," Indonesian Commercial Newsletter (22 May 1995).

Staff. "Press schedule of the trip of Vice President Gore and Deputy President," US Newswire (10 July 1996).

Staff. "Pudjiadi Prestige to develop the Marbella residential condominium resort on Anyer beach in West Java," Indonesia Times (4 October 1994), p. 3.

Staff. "Pulse: Plans Texas retail and entertainment complex," Engineering News Record (11 July 1994), p. 37.

Staff. "Vice President [Gore] and South African Deputy President visit Baltimore," The Associated Press Political Service (22 July 1996).

Staff. "Civil Lawsuits," Arizona Business Gazette (13 May 1999), p. 6.

ULI Staff. "From country store to cybercade: The past, present & future of shopping center development," Urban Land Institute (May 1997).

Ullman, R. "CocoWalk stimulating business in the Grove—Building of the Month," The Miami Herald (14 April 1991).

Uricchio, M. "Malling around, touring today's upscale shopping centers," Pittsburgh Post Gazette Magazine (6 July 1989), pp. 15,17.

Vazquez, L. "Glen Oak's Mays yielding to stylish mall," The New York Times (17 July 1988).

Whitehouse Staff. "Whitehouse Administration," Washington Agenda (22 July 1996).

Acknowledgements

Our group is about problem solving—using design to provide answers, and to create places that very special clients and their audiences can enjoy. I firmly believe that appropriate design adds value, not just in an economic sense, but also by crafting places that people value as "theirs," which adds to their quality of life. Thanks first and foremost to our talented and diverse group for its extraordinary ability to create unique places that resonate with vitality.

Congratulations also to several people who were instrumental in producing this impressive publication. Special thanks to MJ Dame, who coordinated the publication process. His tireless work, sincere dedication, creativity, and diplomacy are what made this book possible. Particularly noteworthy was his tenacity in uncovering, locating, rediscovering, collating, and preparing the visual history of our group and work. Thank you, MJ.

Thanks also to writer Rick Bader, whose thoughtful questions, insightful observations, and no-nonsense manner of writing helped us weave together Design Group's interesting and sometimes turbulent story.

Thanks to Valerie Knauff, who heads our in-house graphics team, for her patience, her humor, and most of all her ability to create designs that met the decidedly conflicting instructions and opinions she was given by my partners and associates.

I greatly appreciate the efforts of the many talented photographers who contributed to the book. In particular, I would like to acknowledge the creative, globe-trotting work of Tim Griffith and, locally, Maryland photographer Walter Larimore, who went beyond the call of duty to produce outstanding work.

Without the trust, confidence, and inspiration of our clients, at home and overseas, none of this would be possible—thanks to you, all from Baltimore to Bali, Cape Town to Cairo.

Sincere thanks to The Images Publishing Group, Ltd for this opportunity to showcase our work. We are indeed honored.

Roy Higgs

CEO

Al Ghurair Group: 25 (6–8)

Bahgat Group: 167 (10)

David Brazier: 32 (1)

Arturo DeCastro: 209 (5)

Thomas Delbeck: 74 (1); 75 (4,5)

Carlos Diniz: 119 (3)

Stanley Doctor Architectural Perspectives: 54 (1); 55 (5); 63 (4,6); 143 (6)

Einzig Photographers: 138 (2); 139 (3); 140 (4–7); 141 (8,9)

Dan Forer Photographer: 27 (2); 28 (3); 29 (9); 30 (11,13,14); 31 (16–18)

Jeremy Green: 82 (2,3); 83 (4); 84 (7); 85 (9–11); 98 (2); 116 (2,3); 117 (5); 184 (4)

Tim Griffith: 24 (4); 76 (1,2); 78 (10); 79 (11–14); 112 (2); 113 (5); 120 (1); 121 (3); 122 (5); 123 (6,8–10); 156 (1); 157 (4,5); 186 (2); 188 (7,9); 189 (11); 203 (1,3); 204 (2); 206 (4,5); 207 (7,8); 211 (1,4); 212 (1); 213 (4); 214 (5); 215 (7,8); 216 (1); 217 (3); 219 (8–10)

Peter Hasselman: 126 (1,2,4,5); 163 (2–7)

Steve Hogben Architectural Photographics: 44 (1–3); 45 (4)

Izzet Kehribar: 22 (1,3); 23 (4)

Walter Larrimore: 34 (1,3); 35 (4); 54 (2,3); 57 (4); 66 (2); 67 (5); 68 (7); 70 (2); 83 (5,6); 87 (4); 88 (1,2); 89 (3); 91 (5–10); 92 (11–13); 93 (14); 94 (17–19); 95 (20); 98 (3,4); 100 (1,2); 102 (2); 103 (5–7); 108 (7–10); 125 (4,5); 136 (1); 137 (4–6); 162 (1); 164 (2); 165 (1); 166 (3); 167 (9); 168 (1,2); 169 (3–5); 170 (2); 171 (1,2); 176 (2); 178 (1); 185 (6); 187 (4); 198 (1–3); 199 (5–7,9); 200 (10); 220 (1); 221 (2,4–6); 227 (1)

Ronnie Levitan Photography: 18 (1,2); 19 (6); 20 (7,9); 21 (10,12,13); 33 (3,5); 36 (3); 37 (6,8); 63 (7); 70 (1); 71 (3); 72 (4,5); 73 (9–11); 132 (1); 133 (3,6); 143 (3,4); 158 (3)

Roger Miller: 236

Muvico Theaters: 51 (1–3,4,5); 52 (7); 64 (1,2); 65 (1–3); 146 (1–3); 147 (5,7); 149 (11,13)

Old Mutual Properties: 62 (3); 63 (5)

Oliveros & Friends: 66 (1); 67 (3,4); 118 (2); 119 (5); 151 (6); 175 (4); 181 (7–10); 184 (1–3); 185 (5); 186 (1); 188 (5); 209 (7)

PT. Pujiadi Prestige: 204 (1)

PT. Kahuripan Raya: 186 (3); 188 (8); 189 (10)

Salim Group: 179 (1)

Steinkamp/Ballogg: 38 (2); 39 (3–6); 40 (7,8); 41 (10,11,13,14)

All uncredited photographs, illustrations, renderings, sketches, models and images reproduced in this monograph © copyright Development Design Group, Inc.

Index

Bold page numbers refer to projects
included in Selected and Current Works

Development Design Group, Inc.

7 Saint Paul Street

Baltimore, Maryland 21202

410 962 0505

410 783 0816

web: www.ddg-usa.com

e-mail: ddg@ddg-usa.com